THE GENERALIST COUNSEL

The Generalist Counsel

How Leading General Counsel Are Shaping Tomorrow's Companies

Prashant Dubey
Eva Kripalani

Oxford University Press is a department of the University of Oxford. It furthers the University's objective of excellence in research, scholarship, and education by publishing worldwide.

Oxford New York
Auckland Cape Town Dar es Salaam Hong Kong Karachi Kuala Lumpur Madrid
Melbourne Mexico City Nairobi New Delhi Shanghai Taipei Toronto

With offices in
Argentina Austria Brazil Chile Czech Republic France Greece Guatemala Hungary
Italy Japan Poland Portugal Singapore South Korea Switzerland Thailand
Turkey Ukraine Vietnam

Published in the United States of America by
Oxford University Press
198 Madison Avenue, New York, NY 10016

Library of Congress Cataloging-in-Publication Data

Dubey, Prashant.
The generalist counsel : how leading general counsel are shaping tomorrow's companies /
Prashant Dubey, Eva Kripalani.
pages cm.
Includes bibliographical references and index.
ISBN 978-0-19-989235-8 (pbk. : alk. paper)
1. Corporate lawyers—United States. I. Kripalani, Eva. II. Title.
KF1425.D83 2013
346.73'066023—dc23

2013009682

---

15 14 13 12 11

Printed in the United States of America on acid-free paper

Note to Readers
This publication is designed to provide accurate and authoritative information in regard to the subject matter covered. It is based upon sources believed to be accurate and reliable and is intended to be current as of the time it was written. It is sold with the understanding that the publisher is not engaged in rendering legal, accounting, or other professional services. If legal advice or other expert assistance is required, the services of a competent professional person should be sought. Also, to confirm that the information has not been affected or changed by recent developments, traditional legal research techniques should be used, including checking primary sources where appropriate.

(Based on the Declaration of Principles jointly adopted by a Committee of the American Bar Association and a Committee of Publishers and Associations.)

Dedicated to all the legal professionals
who tirelessly strive to add value to the
companies they serve

Contents

Introduction

"I realized that something dramatic was happening within the corporate law department. That is where innovation and leadership of the legal profession was going on. The reason I accepted an in-house position was because I didn't see the law firm as the place where innovation would happen anymore."

P.D. VILLARREAL, *Senior Vice President, Global Litigation, GlaxoSmithKline*[1]

The rapid pace at which corporate legal departments have changed in the past few decades is a topic several legal scholars have addressed as the position, influence, and purview of the corporate lawyer—in particular, that of the General Counsel—has evolved and continues to do so.[2] The majority of these writings has focused on the areas of independence and ethics and the special challenges General Counsel face in effectively performing the "gatekeeping" role.[3] However, we have found relatively

1. Unless otherwise noted, quotations are from interviews with identified interviewees.

2. See Carl D. Liggio, *The Changing Role of Corporate Counsel*, 46 Emory L. J. 1201 (1997) [hereinafter Liggio, *The Changing Role*]; Carl D. Liggio, Sr., *A Look at the Role of Corporate Counsel: Back to the Future—or Is It the Past?* 44 Ariz. L. Rev. 621 (2002) [hereinafter Liggio, *Back to the Future*]; Deborah A. DeMott, *The Discrete Roles of General Counsel*, 74 Fordham L. Rev. 955 (2005). See also, E. Norman Veasey & Christine T. Di Guglielmo, *Indispensable Counsel* (Oxford University Press 2011) [hereinafter *Indispensable Counsel*].

3. See Omari Scott Simmons & James D. Dinnage, *Innkeepers: A Unifying Theory of the In-House Counsel Role*, 41 Seton Hall Law Review 77, 81 (2011).

little written about the career paths and experiences of the General Counsel who have been at the forefront of these changes. In particular, we were interested in understanding more about how some of today's successful General Counsel view the role, how they attained it, and the skill sets they believe are necessary to be successful once they are there.

It seems clear that successfully executing one's role as General Counsel requires a significantly broader skill set than that associated with the traditional image of the "top lawyer" in a company. Today, CEOs and other business leaders look to the General Counsel for far more than legal advice. Businesses today have much greater expectations from the position than they once did, which has made the position both more interesting and more challenging. We have used the term "Generalist Counsel" to describe where we believe the General Counsel position has evolved today in U.S. corporations and in global corporations with significant operations in the United States.

Today, leading General Counsel are sought out by their peers on the senior leadership team for strategic input to decisions that will move the business forward. In fact, it is our observation that in many companies key business innovations are resulting from strategies put forth by General Counsel and their leadership teams. Fulfilling these expectations has required that today's successful General Counsel develop competencies in areas fairly recently thought to be the province of other members of the corporate leadership team. As Hilary Krane, Vice President and General Counsel of NIKE, Inc., said about her previous role as General Counsel of Levi Strauss: "Once there, I realized [the General Counsel role] is not just about fire prevention and fire fighting—it is being a part of a team that is trying to run and grow a multinational business. You are a senior executive jointly charged with creating, nurturing, and projecting a sustainable future."

We have also observed that the rapid pace at which the General Counsel role has evolved has shone a bright light on law firms, which by contrast, have appeared relatively slow to change. There has been considerable discussion about the unwillingness of law firms to adapt their business models to address some of the changes that are occurring in the legal profession, as well as the needs being voiced by this new breed of General Counsel. This tendency toward slow response by law firms has also been chronicled by distinguished experts, in some cases resulting in stark predictions about their inevitable demise.[4] Though there have always been differences between the practice of law in a law firm and serving in an in-house role, the divide has widened as the role and influence of the General Counsel position has continued to expand well beyond a traditional legal role. This has exacerbated some of the tensions that exist between General Counsel and outside counsel—a relationship that should be very important to both sides.

We have also observed that many lawyers who have sought to innovate within the confines of the law firm have become frustrated by the constraints. Some, like P.D. Villarreal, whose statement about innovation is used to open this introduction, have found a more hospitable environment in the corporate legal department. There, it seems that lawyers often experience more freedom to innovate than they have known before, and the successful ones run with it.

What does it mean to go beyond "traditional lawyering?" What precipitated the need for this shift to a more expansive skill set? Are lawyerly skills still important? What happened to just being "the buck stops here" risk adjudicator? What does this mean for the future of the General Counsel? How does one successfully

4. See Richard Susskind, *The End of Lawyers? Rethinking the Nature of Legal Services* (Oxford University Press, 2008).

execute the role of a General Counsel with the bar shifting in shape, height, and composition? These are some of the questions we wanted to ask.

Through research and in-depth interviews with sitting and former General Counsel and executives in the sphere of influence of the General Counsel, we have had an opportunity to ask these questions. In the process, we have identified the existence of a deliberate evolution in the fabric and tenor of the role of a General Counsel. *The Generalist Counsel* chronicles this evolution, bringing it to life with examples from the careers of many who have been the change makers. We recount for readers the frustrations of some as they chafed under the more restrictive culture of the law firm. We share the sometimes harsh lessons learned after these now-successful executives made the transition to an in-house role and were developing the skills they would need. We chronicle some of their "Aha!" moments as these innovators (most of whom spent significant time in law firms) shifted from a reactive stance to a proactive one focused on how they could help the company not only achieve but also shape its business objectives. We describe how they experienced more career satisfaction, increased influence, and respect within their organizations. We also share personal stories of some of these "larger than life" personalities—stories that provide context for how these General Counsel execute their role today but are also just very interesting from a human-interest perspective. Sometimes a story's only purpose is to entertain, and most certainly, the accomplished individuals we interviewed at length for this book are—in addition to many other things—entertaining.

The Generalist Counsel also discusses how this shift is leading to other innovations within the legal profession being driven by today's successful corporate legal departments. These include changes in relationships with outside counsel, as well as products and services today's General Counsel demand to more effectively support them in their role.

At its core, this book is principally about recognizing and chronicling the legitimacy, importance, and strategic influence of a corporate executive who we believe is shaping how corporations are built, managed, grown, and governed.

Welcome... Generalist Counsel.

1

The Generalist Counsel Emerges

"A General Counsel needs to be a business person first and a lawyer second—not a lawyer that understands the business, but a business person that happens to be a lawyer."

MARLA PERSKY, *Senior Vice President, General Counsel, and Corporate Secretary, Boehringher Ingelheim Corporation*

A Brief Historical Perspective

The term "General Counsel" has been used for decades, predominantly in the United States, to describe the top lawyer in a corporation or other nonlaw firm entity. In many organizations, this term is used interchangeably with "Chief Legal Officer."[1]

The early history of the General Counsel role in American business has been chronicled extensively as one in which the General Counsel's star rose and then fell, with the position enjoying great prestige in the late nineteenth and early twentieth centuries, only to experience a decline as the twentieth century progressed.[2] By the 1940s, the General Counsel role had significantly diminished in importance, while the role of other

1. Sarah Helene Duggin, *The Pivotal Role of the General Counsel in Promoting Corporate Integrity and Professional Responsibility*, 51 St. Louis U. L.J. 989, 991 (2007), (Duggin notes that "'Chief legal officer' is also the terminology used by the Securities and Exchange Commission (SEC) in its Standards of Professional Conduct for Attorneys Appearing and Practicing Before the Commission in the Representation of an Issuer, 17 C.F.R. § 205 (2003).").

2. *Id.* at 995; see also Liggio, *Back to the Future,* Introduction, *supra* note 2, at 1201. See also, Veasey & Guglielmo, *Indispensable Counsel,* Introduction, *supra* note 2, at 27–38.

business executives, particularly those in marketing and finance, expanded significantly.[3] The General Counsel had been relegated to that of a "relatively minor management figure, stereotypically, a lawyer from the corporation's principal outside law firm who had not quite made the grade as partner."[4] The responsibilities of the General Counsel had become limited to handling "routine matters of corporate housekeeping and (unsurprisingly) to serving as liaison between members of management and counsel's former law firm [with] service as senior management's trusted adviser or as a monitor of how well outside counsel performed [falling] outside of the general counsel's portfolio."[5]

During this period, it is probably fair to say that, at best, the General Counsel position provided some level of comfort for top management when forced to wade into legal waters with these "inferior" lawyers providing some degree of "lawyerly knowledge" about legal issues facing the company (usually litigation). It is also fair to say that the General Counsel and the other in-house lawyers were often perceived as a necessary evil begrudgingly indulged by the company's nonlawyers, but who were not viewed as "adding value."

Based on the results of our interviews, these perceptions are hardly ancient history. Until fairly recently in many companies, the General Counsel and the legal department were often perceived as the "business prevention group" rather than contributors to the success of the business. At best, the legal department was considered a necessary stop along the journey in completing business transactions, often brought into business discussions at

3. See DeMott, Introduction, *supra* note 2, at 959 ("By the 1940s, '[t]he new wunderkinds of the business community were marketing and finance types—the MBAs'") (quoting from Liggio, *Back to the Future,* Introduction, supra note 2, at 621).

4. Abram Chayes & Antonia H. Chayes, *Corporate Counsel and the Elite Law Firm*, 37 Stan. L. Rev. 277 (1985).

5. DeMott, Introduction, *supra* note 2, at 959.

the end to add the "legal blessing" to a negotiation and/or to be a scrivener of contract terms that had already been negotiated by the "business people." Frequently, even the function of signing off on already-determined business decisions was actually performed by outside counsel, with the General Counsel serving as a "rolodex lawyer" who summoned these subject-matter expert law firm lawyers any time the need for legal work arose. This reinforced the view of many that inferior lawyers fulfilled the role of the General Counsel and other in-house counsel.

Most of our interviewees had some experience dealing with these perceptions and, in some instances, all too recently. MardiLyn Saathoff, Vice President of Legal, Risk and Compliance at NW Natural Gas Company, a publicly traded utility based in Portland, Oregon, had this comment about how businesses have historically perceived the role of their in-house lawyers: "There was a time when the perception within companies was that the really good lawyers were all in law firms. As for the in-house lawyers, the view was that we sort of have to have them, but no one was really sure what they did. And I think we still battle that perception at times."

Reporting relationships and compensation often reflected the diminished importance of the General Counsel role. It was not uncommon for General Counsel to report to an executive below the CEO in the corporate hierarchy—often the CFO—meaning that the General Counsel did not sit at the highest level of company leadership. This was reflected in the General Counsel's compensation as well as the compensation of other members of the legal team.[6]

Not surprisingly, as the General Counsel's star was falling, there was a corresponding ascendancy in the reputation and

6. See Liggio, *The Changing Rule*, Introduction, *supra* note 2, at 1202 (noting that the ratio of General Counsel compensation to the compensation of the CEO had fallen from a high of 65% during the "golden years" of the 1920s and 1930s to a low of approximately 30% by the mid-1970s.)

purview of outside law firms. Filling the void that the decline of the General Counsel role had left, "Wall Street lawyers and their counterparts in other cities fashioned a role for themselves as trusted advisors who would guide their clients through the complex web of problems at the intersection of law and business."[7] The relationships among large corporate clients and their law firms—often a single firm—were "long and enduring" and "extended to every aspect of the company's business."[8] Among other things, this had the effect of enabling law firms to attract and retain the best and the brightest lawyers.[9] In sum, really good lawyers tended to stay in law firms and become successful partners, where compensation and other opportunities were often perceived to be superior to those offered to in-house lawyers.

Things Begin to Change

During the 1970s and 1980s, a number of events occurred that led to a greater appreciation of the role of the General Counsel.[10] There was a significant increase in merger and acquisition activity, public offerings, and other business transactions. Transactions became increasingly more complex and involved greater risks, financial and otherwise. Government regulation and oversight by a proliferation of regulatory organizations at both the federal and state level created a maze of regulatory activity through which corporations now had to navigate. The volume of business litigation grew

7. David B. Wilkins, *Team of Rivals? Toward a New Model of the Corporate Attorney-Client Relationship*, 78 Fordham L. Rev. 2067, 2077 (2010).

8. *Id.*

9. DeMott, Introduction, *supra* note 2, at 959.

10. See Liggio, *The Changing Role*, Introduction, *supra* note 2, at 1203–1204. See also DeMott, *The Discrete Roles*, Introduction, *supra* note 2, at 960–961.

exponentially during this period, with high profile litigation instituted by and against corporations becoming much more common, including class actions and derivative suits. And all of these activities, coupled with the escalating costs of legal services outside law firms provided, resulted in significant increases in legal expenses.

As these changes evolved, companies began to realize the value of the General Counsel's role in helping them understand and navigate through the increasingly more complex risk management and corporate governance landscape that had become a necessary part of doing business. Corporations responded by increasing the size of their legal departments and the quality of their lawyers.[11]

It is interesting that one of the factors contributing to the rise of the General Counsel was outside counsel becoming a victim of its own success. According to one source, "[e]scalating legal costs, coupled with a distaste for lawyers generally, were a critical catalyst in propelling employed counsel into the forefront of the modern corporate hierarchy. This phenomenon [was] compounded by a distrust that many CEOs and chief financial officers (CFOs) [felt] for the retained bar."[12]

An early milestone in the resurgence of the power of the General Counsel occurred in 1982 with the formation of the American Corporate Counsel Association (ACCA). This was an overt sign that in-house counsel and their leadership were increasing their influence in organizations. Renamed the Association of Corporate Counsel (ACC) in 2003, the advocacy role this organization assumed indicated the need for General Counsel to more formally represent their growing influence and scope of responsibility in not just providing legal advice to their organizations,

11. Liggio, *The Changing Role,* Introduction, *supra* note 2, at 1203–1204.

12. *Id.*

but in also helping execute business strategies that were critical to the company's success. This view is supported by the following statement from Gray Castle, a former General Counsel of Xerox, Cigna, and The Mutual Life Insurance Company of New York, as well as a former partner in more than one major law firm, which appears on ACC's website: "[We needed] a national organization, especially one that would help raise the sights of in-house counsel and provide a unified voice for our profession." At this writing, the ACC has more than 30,000 members from more than 10,000 organizations in seventy-five countries.

The formation of ACC was followed by efforts from the organized bar to address the needs of corporate counsel. Suddenly, state bar associations formed corporate counsel committees and the American Bar Association (ABA) formed several new committees specifically for corporate counsel, as well as committees designed to encourage collaboration between inside and outside counsel.[13]

Another Transformation

No discussion about the evolution of the General Counsel role would be complete without acknowledging the contributions of Ben Heineman, who served as General Electric Company's Senior Vice President and Chief Legal Officer from 1987 to 2005.[14] Though we did not have the privilege of interviewing Mr. Heineman, much has been written about his illustrious career and, among other things, he is often credited with leading yet another period of transformation in the role and stature of in-house legal departments.

13. See Liggio, *The Changing Role,* Introduction, *supra* note 2, at 1211–1212.

14. See Tanina Rostain, *General Counsel In the Age of Compliance, Preliminary Findings and New Research Questions,* 21 Georgetown Journal of Legal Ethics, 465, 471 (2008) (noting that Heineman represented "the model of the new in-house counsel" and that, under his leadership, the legal department at GE "took on the feel of an elite law firm.").

Heineman was managing partner of the Washington office of Sidley & Austin, focusing on Supreme Court and test case litigation, when he decided to go to General Electric. As he commented in a 2006 article for *Corporate Counsel Magazine*, he was by no means the first distinguished lawyer to leave a lucrative and well-respected law firm practice to go in-house, but he did pioneer a new vision for in-house legal departments:

> What distinguished GE was not going outside for its General Counsel, but going outside for many of his colleagues: the commitment—not just of the GC, but of GE's CEO, Jack Welch, and his successor, Jeff Immelt—to redefine the role of inside counsel, to drive the highest-quality lawyers across the top of the company, and to build a cohort of legal talent just below the top that could advance upward in the company as the years passed.[15]

"Ben Heineman became the symbol of the modern general counsel who helped to unravel the close connection between law firms and corporate clients that Cravath pioneered."[16] Heineman recruited lawyers from the nation's top law firms to work in GE's legal department, and they began to take back much of the work that had previously been sent to outside counsel.

One of the lawyers recruited to Mr. Heineman's elite team at GE was Jeff Kindler.[17] Kindler made the well-publicized leap from Williams & Connolly to GE in 1990, which attracted the

15. Ben W. Heineman, Jr., *In the Beginning*, Law.com, May 1, 2006, http://www.law.com/corporatecounsel/PubArticleCC.jsp?id=900005450428&In_the_Beginning.

16. Wilkins, Ch. 1, *supra* note 11, at 2081.

17. Jeff Kindler's career is explored in more detail in Chapters Two and Eight. Among the positions he held were General Counsel of McDonald's Corporation and Pfizer, Inc. He also served as Pfizer's Chairman and CEO from 2006 to 2010.

attention of lawyers at major firms everywhere.[18] Kindler was considered a superstar litigator. He earned his J.D. in 1980 from Harvard, *magna cum laude,* and his B.A. in 1977 from Tufts University, *summa cum laude.* After a brief stint at the Federal Communications Commission, he joined Williams & Connolly, a premier law firm, where he became a partner. Kindler had only recently become a partner when GE approached him. He told us that he was getting great work and "loved what he did." He described Williams & Connolly as a "fantastic" law firm from which people rarely left. As he put it, "at that time, going in-house was the furthest thing from my mind." He referred to the comments he had heard from his law firm colleagues about lawyers who went in-house, including their labeling of them as "rolodex lawyers," and said that he and his colleagues firmly believed that CEOs and business leaders continued to look to outside counsel for important advice.

But then Kindler heard Heineman explain his vision for the legal department at GE. Heineman saw GE as a place where the in-house lawyers would do the interesting and important work. Heineman told Kindler that GE's in-house counsel would have autonomy and direct accountability to the business and that their career growth and compensation opportunities would be competitive with those offered by a law firm. Persuaded by Heineman's vision, Kindler decided to make the leap. He acknowledges that many of his colleagues openly questioned his decision. However, it didn't take him long to realize it had been the right decision for him.

P.D. Villarreal was one of those successful law firm partners who was intrigued by the Kindler move and soon became part of

18. Interview with P.D. Villarreal, Senior Vice President, Global Litigation, GlaxoSmith-Kline (2011).

the cadre of exceptional lawyers comprising GE's in-house legal department. Villarreal shared this story about how he arrived at GE in 1995:

> I became a partner at Sonnenschein Nath & Rosenthal in Chicago in 1983. I loved the firm, including the fact that they did a lot of pro bono work in the community.
>
> One day I was taking the train into the city and reading an American Lawyer cover article on Jeff Kindler. I remember thinking he sounded quite different from the corporate lawyers I was used to working with, and I was intrigued. Later that morning, an executive recruiter called me about a Fortune 500 company position. I was about to hang up when he said the company was GE and Jeff Kindler would be my boss.
>
> He told me that Kindler wanted to meet for drinks in Chicago. Although I had no intention of leaving the firm, I knew I had to meet with him. Well, Jeff is extremely charismatic and persuasive. Two weeks after I met him, I was in Fairfield, CT, meeting with other members of the GE team and buying a house. That was it.

P.D. Villarreal is an industry stalwart with a demonstrated talent for being able to see in places where the light may not yet be shining its brightest. As his statement at the opening of our introduction reflects, he saw leadership of the profession shifting from law firms to the corporate legal department. And Kindler and the other people he met at GE were at the epicenter of that shift.

This shift in leadership of the profession mirrored the shift to the General Counsel's leadership role in the business. By the mid-1990s, General Counsel were more frequently reporting directly to the CEO and regularly assuming a place at the leadership table with the CFO and line of business leaders.[19] Today, General Counsel have an expectation that they will execute their role as members of the senior leadership team. As Krane said when describing her tenure as General Counsel at Levi-Strauss: "I was proactively involved in [business discussions] throughout. If the GC did not sit on the worldwide leadership team, I would have said no thanks to the role."

CEOs and other business leaders had become increasingly aware of the benefits to the company of having the General Counsel understand and be more involved in the business. As a result, General Counsel were made aware of strategic initiatives earlier and were able to weigh in with their viewpoints to shape decision making, based on their roles not just as risk managers but also as executives knowledgeable about the business.[20]

Changing Rewards

Other talented lawyers from the nation's leading law firms saw these opportunities, and the number of lawyers migrating from law firm to in-house positions increased as many left their firms to assume these more lucrative and challenging positions. As more of these transitions occurred, other professional associations targeting General Counsel began to emerge. In 1998, the Corporate Executive Board, which had long provided guidance to CFOs and CEOs in the form of best practice research, initiated the General Counsel Roundtable (GCR) in response to the

19. See Rostain, Ch. 1, *supra* note 14, at 473.

20. See Duggin, Ch. 1, *supra* note 1, at 1015 (discussing the reasons for and the importance of involving general counsel in the strategic planning process).

demand of General Counsel for similar resources. GCR describes its origins on its website:

> The Legal Practice was conceived in 1998, after several General Counsel approached the Corporate Executive Board, requesting that we extend our brand of practical, business-focused research, facilitated network discussion, and information exchange to the challenges facing the Legal function.

There were conferences and other networking opportunities (in addition to those traditionally sponsored by law firms as business development strategies) where General Counsel could focus on the myriad issues facing in-house legal departments and share best practices as CFOs and CEOs had been doing for many years. These resources included those designed to assist the General Counsel in understanding risk assessment, technology, finance, and other business issues rather than substantive legal content.

With respect to these developments, NW Natural's MardiLyn Saathoff commented:

> I recognized many years ago that the role of the General Counsel [was] definitely evolving. The emergence of networking groups, websites and other resources targeting General Counsel and in-house legal departments was evidence of that. You wouldn't have seen so many resources develop if the role were not evolving.

The compensation of General Counsel has increased commensurate with this recognition of their expanded role, often putting them into the illustrious category of the most highly compensated executives in a company.[21] And their compensation

21. Broc Romanek, *How Much Does a GC Make? Equilar's General Counsel Pay Study* Blog Post, The Corporate Counsel.net, November 7, 2012, http://www.thecorporatecounsel.net/Blog/2012/11/how-much-does-a-gc-make-equilars-general-counsel-pay-study.html.

continues to rise. In fact, despite a recent dip in compensation as of this writing, the average cash compensation of the top 100 General Counsel has increased by seventy percent between 2002 and 2012.[22]

It has been our observation that today's successful General Counsel blend mastery of disciplines such as finance, technology, business analytics, and communications with substantive legal knowledge. They also demonstrate leadership skills, given the much broader expectations of the General Counsel's leadership of core company functions. In many organizations, the General Counsel's role has been expanded to include functions traditionally managed outside the legal department, including corporate development, risk management, compliance, governance, government relations, corporate communications, and more.

For those General Counsel who aspire to expand their roles and/or cross over into the business side of the company, there is a need to understand how to position themselves to attain these roles and how to be successful in executing them. The encouraging news is that their training as lawyers provides a solid foundation from which to acquire those additional skills and achieve their goals. And we hope that the guidance offered in this book by those who have already traveled this path is helpful.

22. The 2012 GC Compensation Survey, *Corporate Counsel*, August 1, 2012, http://www.law.com/corporatecounsel/PubArticleCC.jsp?id=1341783741529&thepage=1.

2

Shaping the Path

"Everything I learned about being a General Counsel, I learned in school."

ALLEN WAXMAN, *Senior Vice President and General Counsel, Eisai Inc., and former General Counsel, Pfizer Inc.*

The story doesn't go exactly as this quote would imply. Allen Waxman, who is soft spoken, warm, and personable, may be misread by some as timid. This would be a mistake. He has had an illustrious career as a litigator and also as the chief legal officer at the largest pharmaceutical company in the world. He is presently General Counsel at an innovative pharmaceutical company, Eisai Inc. So, did a high achiever like Waxman really learn how to be a successful General Counsel in school? Well, in a way, yes.

Waxman was a high-powered litigator at Williams & Connolly when he was recruited to Pfizer's in-house legal department in 2003. Upon Jeff Kindler's ascension from General Counsel to CEO of Pfizer, Waxman was promoted to the General Counsel position. He credits his ability to secure this position, as well as to perform his duties as General Counsel, in large part to the experiences he had while helping to build the Thurgood Marshall Academy Public Charter High School.

While a partner at Williams & Connolly in the 1990s, Waxman read about an effort by some law students to start a public charter high school. He wanted to learn more about this initiative, so he reached out to its champion, Josh Kern, who was then a student at Georgetown University Law School. Lesson one: a twelve-year veteran of a major law firm reaches out to a third-year law student and requests a meeting. If Waxman had allowed his ego to get in the way, he would never have gotten involved. After speaking to Kern and learning more about his efforts, Waxman knew he wanted to help support the cause and requested a follow-up meeting with Kern. With Waxman's help, Kern eventually secured a charter school license and established the Thurgood Marshall Academy Public Charter High School. This is when Waxman's real General Counsel training began.

Waxman said that every day brought a new challenge and presented questions that were multidimensional. He had to understand how to work with educators and other subject-matter experts on the board in a collaborative way, as well as answer for himself a number of important questions:

- How do you build a program responsibly when the stakes are so high—children, their education, and their futures lie in the balance?
- How can the school be properly financed? The school received a certain amount per student from the school district but could not scale up fast enough to have the number of students needed to break even.
- How could he get the entire legal community involved?
- How could he execute his duties efficiently and still work in a team? Could he continue to check his ego at the door?

Waxman said that traversing all of these challenges and making decisions while balancing risk and outcome was the best management training he could have hoped for. He credits this experience, in large part, with providing him the skills and battlefield experience he needed to secure and succeed in the role of General Counsel.

How Others Shaped the Seat

In this chapter, we explore how some other successful General Counsel secured their positions—how they prepared themselves for achieving the roles and the career milestones that led to their eventual ascension to the Chief Legal Officer position. As Waxman's story illustrates, the pathway is not always a traditional one. We also highlight some common themes in these varied stories—themes that are meant to provide perspective to aspiring General Counsel and assist them in charting their own course to the seat.

Responders and Creators

In terms of general patterns, we observed that General Counsel were either responders or creators. In other words, in shaping their pathways to the GC seat, these individuals either responded to opportunities presented to them (informally or formally) or they created their own opportunities. An important point to be made here is that neither approach was reactive—even responders proactively responded to opportunities. We also found that responders sometimes evolved into creators but that creators rarely became responders. As with any model, there are no absolutes—the observed patterns occurred along a continuum. This also has the convenient effect of allowing us to create a two-by-two matrix, without which any business book would not be worth the weight of the ink on its pages. This matrix is what we call—The GC Career Model (Figure 1).

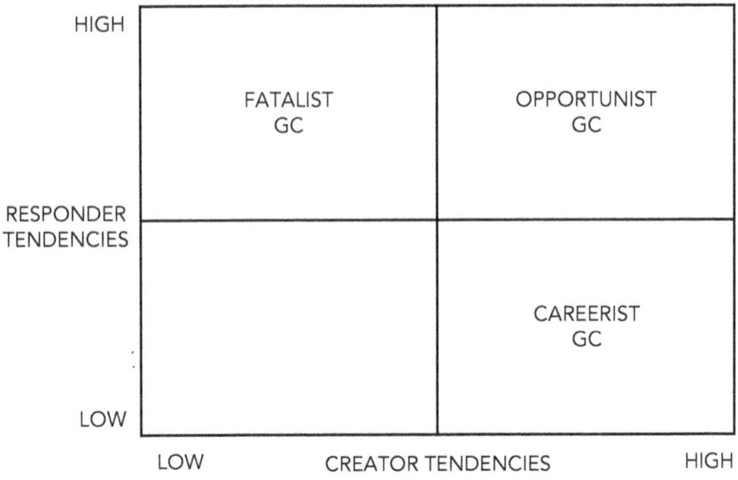

HIGH

FATALIST GC

OPPORTUNIST GC

RESPONDER TENDENCIES

CAREERIST GC

LOW

LOW CREATOR TENDENCIES HIGH

FIGURE 1

GC Career Model.

Co-opting Labels

In our quest to describe how General Counsel shaped the seats they eventually occupied, we tried our best to avoid labels. It is our experience that labels tend to get overused, and it is too easy to draw summary conclusions from simple words or phrases. However, after this futile exercise, and after conducting our own risk-value analysis, we settled on labels that are traditionally used in a pejorative context. This was odd, and almost ironic. Apparently, the available vocabulary did not allow us to find "feel good" labels for the pathways of the professionals we profiled, so we co-opted other terms. We will endeavor to explain the rationale behind our use of these terms, all of which are intended in a positive context.

Fatalist

Fatalists are typically known for their belief that all events are predetermined by fate and therefore unalterable. Furthermore, conventional definitions of fatalists also paint them with a brush of powerlessness, reflecting a general belief that a fatalist thinks he or she is powerless to change his or her destiny.

In our model, we have co-opted this term but altered it to define a category of General Counsel who have not blindly meandered their way to the Chief Legal Officer seat but have proactively responded to opportunities that were presented to them with an inevitability fatalists assume—opportunities that they would argue were fated to be present and destined to be theirs.

As such, a *Fatalist GC* is one who shaped, rather than changed, his or her destiny by proactively responding to the opportunities that he or she felt were the right ones.

An Example of a Fatalist GC

A good metaphor for a fatalist approach to shaping the General Counsel pathway is to think about something that is elusive to many people—ballroom dancing. Ballroom dancing can be the graceful, free flowing movements of the waltz; the expressive and sensuous emanations of the Latin rhythm; or the powerful, drama-infused moves of the tango. In each case, the idea is to *respond* to instinct and let one's body follow the natural rhythms one *creates* through deliberately executing a series of formal steps. Sound confusing? Not to Tom Sabatino, Executive Vice President and General Counsel of Walgreen Co.

We have never seen Sabatino dance, but we suspect he's pretty good at it. After successfully managing the transaction that led to the business combination between Merck Inc. and Schering-Plough (one of the largest pharmaceutical/life sciences acquisitions in recent history), Sabatino decided to learn ballroom dancing. In a way, this is art imitating life... imitating art...

Sabatino grew up in a rural community in the eastern part of Connecticut. He attended a liberal arts college because he wanted to be, in his own words, "a bunch of different things," so a classic liberal arts education seemed just the ticket.

As a fatalist—one who creates the foundation for opportunities to be presented to him—a liberal arts education, followed by a law degree, seemed to fit Sabatino quite well. Based on his observation of a family friend who was a lawyer in the small town where he grew up, Sabatino decided he wanted to be a lawyer. After graduation, he started out as a litigator but quickly realized that he was built for a different legal experience. So, he created opportunities to get exposed to the corporate practice of his law firm by highlighting the business-oriented coursework he did at the University of Pennsylvania. As a result, Sabatino was presented the opportunity to work on projects related to the public offerings of companies he described as "Route 128 belt firms in Boston." He proactively responded to these opportunities and in the process charted a course that would define him as one of the best business lawyers in the industry.

Sabatino moved to the bustling Midwest town of Chicago—principally because his wife's family was from Chicago. While working for a mid-sized Chicago firm, he created a local network within which he was known for his business acumen as a lawyer. This was not an accident, and neither was the opportunity that was presented to him to work—as a business lawyer—for Marschall Smith, then Assistant General Counsel of Baxter International.

When Sabatino joined Baxter, he positioned himself as flexible and indefatigable when it came to understanding client needs. When asked in his first week to jump on a plane to visit clients on the East Coast, he did not hesitate. When asked to travel from home for a couple of days every week for an entire year, he did not hesitate. When his clients wanted to teach him the intricacies of the computer purchases they wanted him to support, he expressed his willingness to learn. When the company asked him to move to California to open a branch office at a major specialty medical division of Baxter, he agreed. All this time, he was furthering his reputation as a "businessperson who happened to be a lawyer."

This fatalist was then presented with the opportunity to become the CEO of a small medical device company with $4 million in sales, run by one guy. Sabatino's wife worked for the owner of the company, who called Sabatino "out of the blue," asking him if he was interested in becoming CEO of the company. Sabatino, senior counsel at a multibillion dollar medical device company, decided to make the move. Fatalist move? Definitely. And likely inevitable, given the conditions Sabatino had created leading to the presentation of this opportunity.

Sabatino took full advantage of the learning opportunity this CEO role presented. He played every role "from chief cook to bottle washer" and became facile with all aspects of running and growing a business, more than doubling the size of the company in just a few years. He augmented his reputation as someone not afraid to take on things with which he was unfamiliar. When the recession of the early 1990s made it impossible to raise the capital necessary to pursue the company's growth plans, Sabatino began thinking about his next move. Not surprisingly, he was then presented with an opportunity to take on an Associate General Counsel role at American Medical International (AMI), a hospital management company in Dallas, where his former boss, Marschall Smith, was General Counsel. Shortly thereafter, Smith departed AMI and the fatalist General Counsel formally took the seat in his first General Counsel role.

In 1995, AMI was sold, and Sabatino moved back to Chicago to be the General Counsel for the Renal Division of Baxter, one of the largest and most profitable divisions of the company. This led, in 1997, to Sabatino being appointed General Counsel of Baxter International, one of the best-known and most successful companies in the healthcare and medical device industry.

Sabatino was a noted success in this role and executed it successfully for more than six years. He was also intimately involved in leading industry efforts to redefine the role of corporate legal departments in a more strategic way. This, in large part, as well as his ability to manifest these efforts in executing his role at Baxter, led to his appointment as the General Counsel of Schering-Plough, one of the world's largest pharmaceutical companies. Sabatino's business acumen was critical in a consolidating industry—Merck acquired Schering Plough in 2009, and Sabatino's reputation as an M&A and merger integration expert was further bolstered.

In a classic fatalist move, Sabatino then moved back to Chicago from the East Coast and reintegrated into the community that knew him so well. He was presented with the opportunity to become the General Counsel of one of the best-known brands in the world—United Airlines. No surprise—another consolidating industry. When he joined United, the word on the street was that the airline was in the "middle of doing something significant." Soon after, United and Continental Airlines merged, and Sabatino oversaw the transaction.

When his work with United was done, Sabatino decided to move a little farther north in the Chicagoland area and was appointed to his current role as Executive Vice President and General Counsel of Walgreen Co. A few short months after his appointment, Walgreen took a forty-five percent stake in

European pharmacy retailer Alliance Boots for $6.7 billion. Coincidence? Not likely.

Sabatino's career is a perfect example of a Fatalist GC—one where opportunities presented are made inevitable through the careful creation of situations where the presentation of opportunities is unavoidable. However, the key is the fatalist's penchant for responding to these opportunities and fearlessly diving in and immersing himself in unfamiliar domains. Based on Sabatino's success, charting a course as a fatalist may not be such a bad strategy.

Careerist

The term careerist broadly describes a person who has professional advancement as a primary aim. This description should not be interpreted as a criticism—we are not suggesting that a careerist is someone who values success in their career above all else and will seek career advancement by *any* possible means. A career advancement focus is a natural approach to one's work, particularly for lawyers who tend to be competitive and who were likely taught in law school that making partner at a law firm is a measure of professional success. In our model, a Careerist GC is someone who is a creator of opportunity.

In contrast to a Fatalist GC, who shapes his career by *responding* to opportunities presented to him, a Careerist GC is one who creates his own opportunities, with a deliberate plan to shape his career the way *he* has defined it.

There is nothing unseemly about this behavior, and a Careerist GC does not pursue his career with disregard to the implications of his actions—rather, it is our observation that Careerist GC's are careful planners and thoughtful professionals who don't leave much to chance.

Example of a Careerist GC

As defined in our model, in contrast to an Opportunist GC, who responds to opportunities that he may or may not have created, as well as creates opportunities as pathways shape up before him, a careerist is much more deliberate and calibrated. A Careerist GC has a vision for his career and executes strategies to ensure fulfillment of this vision. James Lipscomb, former Executive Vice President and General Counsel of MetLife, Inc., is a Careerist GC.

Lipscomb walked into a hotel room in the Tudor City area of Manhattan impeccably dressed in a deep blue pinstripe suit and flawlessly matching tie. He had the posture of a yoga master, a handshake of steel, and a smile that would cause anyone, however guarded, to drop all defenses. He had retired as the General Counsel of a company with one of the most recognizable brand names in industry—MetLife. Based on Lipscomb's attire, we made the assumption that our interview with him was a stop along his journey for the day and that he obviously had other important matters to tend to in midtown Manhattan that caused him to put on a suit. Our assumption was incorrect.

"James, you didn't have to dress up for us," we said, trying to break the ice. "I know—but I did anyway," said Lipscomb. This is a man with a plan. He is deliberate—even when it comes to dressing in formal business attire for a casual interview. Deliberate may be the best word to describe the pathways James Lipscomb traversed in his almost four decades at MetLife.

"I joined the company [MetLife] right out of law school," Lipscomb said. "That was 1972, and I expected to spend my entire career there as a lawyer, but I did not."

The career path that leads to General Counsel and beyond still typically involves spending time in a law firm, although it is somewhat more common today to see law school graduates go directly in-house. When Lipscomb began his career, going directly in-house was extremely rare for most companies but was more common for larger companies that preferred to train their own people.

Lipscomb became aware of the possibility of going directly in-house from his real property law professor in law school. Lipscomb explained to his professor that he knew he wanted to practice real estate law, even though he had not yet graduated from law school. His professor advised him that he might gain more experience working on the corporate side, given that his objective was to learn all he could about the real estate business. MetLife offered him that opportunity. He joined the company as an attorney in the MetLife Law Department's Real Estate Investments group and worked there with increasing responsibilities for almost eighteen years, moving to the West Coast in the process. He later returned to New York as the leader of the Law Department's Real Estate Investments group—just as he planned.

Visible Accomplishments

One of the most recognizable images in the world is the skyline of New York City. James Lipscomb had a hand in shaping this image. While part of the MetLife Law Department's Real Estate Investments group, he handled the purchase, sale, and financing of many commercial buildings and complexes throughout the United States that now shape the skyline image of many cities, including New York City. As he told us, "my big deal" was in New York City. The building is at 1095 Sixth Avenue in Bryant Park in the heart of midtown Manhattan. When MetLife moved to the building a few years ago, he was the only one in the company who was aware that MetLife had previously owned the building. A self-proclaimed dirt lawyer (more reverently referred to as a real property lawyer), Lipscomb turned his love for buildings and architecture into a career where he became nationally recognized as one of the top real estate lawyers in the United States.

Lipscomb's plan for his career was not self-limiting. His ability as a quick study of people and problems did not go unobserved by the powers that be at MetLife. In 1989, the CEO of MetLife formed a strategy team. "There were ten constituents, five from inside the company and five from outside the company. Participating on this team gave me a top-down view of the company and its businesses," said Lipscomb. To deal with the fallout from the decline of the real estate market in the 1980s, the MetLife CEO asked Lipscomb, because of his real estate knowledge, to join the Real Estate Investment Department to head up the mortgage administration program. "I built my own team," says Lipscomb. "We resolved the problems, and MetLife returned to the mortgage origination market." Of course, Lipscomb was placed in charge of the new mortgage origination team. Again, the Careerist GC was able to chart a course and sail to the next lighthouse.

In the late 1990s, MetLife began preparing to become a public company. Based on his prior experience in the corporate strategy group, Lipscomb was asked by the CEO to head up the Corporate Planning and Strategy group. "I felt that my experience and vision could be more broadly leveraged to drive the company to the next level. I helped lead the effort to prepare the company to become public. My lawyerly discipline, coupled with my knowledge of the company's businesses really came in handy."

Lipscomb had made the transition from recognized real estate lawyer to knowledgeable businessperson within MetLife. When MetLife unexpectedly received the opportunity to purchase another insurance company, part of the purchase included Conning Corporation, a company based in Hartford, Connecticut. The MetLife CEO once again tapped Lipscomb to become the President and CEO of this newly acquired company. "This job involved overseeing its $40–$50 billion asset management portfolio, private equity group, real estate loan origination and servicing platform, equity broker dealer, and insurance industry research group." As a highly regulated business, Conning was in good hands with the deliberate, calibrated leadership of Lipscomb. "Being largely a people business, I felt my mission was to stabilize it, which I did. I managed to preserve the value in the company and then sell the company at a profit for MetLife. This was the culmination of my almost three decades of business and legal experience at MetLife."

After this experience, Lipscomb decided to go back to his lawyer roots—"It was time for me to go back to New York and exercise my lawyerly training." The Careerist GC reentered the corporate legal function as Deputy GC of MetLife. As promised, Lipscomb was appointed General Counsel in 2003, upon the retirement of the previous General Counsel.

James Lipscomb didn't leave much to chance. He didn't control all levers and certainly couldn't orchestrate all environmental factors. However, he planned and executed his career carefully for almost four decades, creating his own opportunities, resolute in his belief that if he focused on making his corporation successful, he himself would attain career success. This is precisely what happened. He was an incredibly business-minded General Counsel—because he was a businessman. He didn't have to imagine himself in the shoes of his clients; he was the client.

"The corporation is all I know," he said.

Lipscomb got the total corporate experience during his thirty-eight years at Met Life, earning a reputation as an expert on the company's many lines of business. Perhaps without realizing it, Lipscomb was setting the standard for what is now expected of the General Counsel at a complex organization.

Lipscomb retired in 2012, having made his mark in innumerable ways. But, as he told us, "the most important thing for me was to establish the example of diversity through inclusion as a corporate strength and a competitive advantage."

Deliberate, career-focused—Careerist GC.

Opportunist

Opportunists are often thought to be people who consciously take selfish advantage of circumstances with little regard for principles or what the consequences are for others. However, in our model, Opportunist GCs are principled people who create opportunities for themselves strategically as well as respond to opportunities presented to them—perhaps presented to them because they themselves played a part in creating the opportunity.

Are these people self-interested? Of course they are—just like any professional seeking career advancement. However, Opportunist GCs are motivated principally by advancing the institutions they serve as well as business and legal practice—a convenient byproduct of these achievements are personal and professional accolades.

An Example of an Opportunist GC

"When I graduated from law school, I couldn't have imagined being the General Counsel of a hamburger company or . . . of Pfizer."

JEFF KINDLER, *former Chairman and CEO of Pfizer, Inc.*

When Jeff Kindler left Williams & Connolly for General Electric, he was, in many ways, responding to an opportunity that he had a hand in creating. Because of his reputation and that of his firm, being contacted by "headhunters" was not unexpected.

He had declined opportunities that had been presented to him before. As he told us: "[Williams & Connolly] was a firm where . . . when you became a partner, you were proud and you stayed. The work was interesting and diverse—we were generalist litigators, thrived on the courtroom—we loved the adversarial system."

In an environment like this, Kindler noted, "the transactional lawyers were the subject matter experts and the litigators were the gladiators—we were expected to be on the outside [of the corporation] not on the inside." This made it all the more surprising when this young partner responded to an opportunity to join the corporate legal department at General Electric. Kindler was among the first of the big-name lawyers to choose the corporation over the firm, and upon his arrival, he immediately began to think of ways to add value to the already talented team in place within General Electric. "When I got there, I set about trying, in as careful and thoughtful a way as I knew how, to be a value-added member of an already high-functioning team."

Daring to be Different

When Kindler arrived at GE, he wasn't there to "throw everything over the wall." Instead, his approach was to build upon a corporate legal strategy put in place by Ben Heineman where outside counsel played a reduced role—essentially reversing the previous order of things. Kindler was tough and very, very smart, a perfect pathfinder for future General Counsel who wanted something more for themselves than handling the more mundane work the in-house attorneys traditionally managed.

One of his first (and most memorable) litigation experiences at GE was to participate as a key member of a team that successfully managed a matter where the Justice Department charged GE for conspiring with DeBeers to fix and raise prices in the worldwide industrial diamond market. This is where opportunism meets serendipity. It was an article about Kindler's participation in the masterful handling of this litigation by a widely heralded team that included well-known lawyers Dan Webb and Bill Baer that P.D. Villarreal was reading when he received the headhunter call about joining GE, as recounted in Chapter One.

How Opportunism Leads to Opportunity

Kindler's opportunistic General Counsel pathway continued when he realized that his job was no longer about rewriting motions that law firms had prepared and determining which depositions to take. "I needed to add value over and above that—to move the business forward," he said. This desire contributed to his furtherance of an innovative and successful litigation avoidance strategy at GE, grounded in Alternative Dispute Resolution (ADR).

Kindler's litigation background and success at GE was a principal reason McDonald's Corporation identified him as a perfect General Counsel candidate when the incumbent General Counsel was ready to retire. McDonald's wanted a General Counsel with a strong litigation background. Kindler provided that and more—he brought best practices from GE to contribute to the legal strategy mix at McDonald's.

The Opportunist GC creates initiative then responds when that initiative stimulates further opportunity.

(Creating the Opportunity) To Get to the Commercial Side of the House

At McDonald's, Jeff Kindler continued on his opportunistic GC path through a business case he formulated during McDonald's acquisition of Boston Market, a restaurant chain that had grown rapidly in the early and mid-1990s but had filed a Chapter 11 bankruptcy in 1998. McDonald's had acquired Boston Market to convert its prime real estate locations into McDonald's stores and was not interested in preserving the Boston Market brand. However, Kindler thought the Boston Market brand still "had legs" and expressed his point of view on branding—certainly not an area typically considered within the purview of a General Counsel at that time. This is not surprising when one considers how Kindler approached every job he held. "I tried my level best to do every job I had as well as I could and to gain broader business experience in order to do that job better, at the same time preparing myself for any future challenges that might arise."

Kindler took part in an effort to convince the CEO of McDonald's to close only a few Boston Market stores, turn some select locations into McDonald's stores, and continue to run the rest as Boston Market locations. Kindler said, "I was then appointed as head of this brand—to put my money where my mouth was." Kindler was made President of Partner Brands and was part of a stellar team that successfully turned Boston Market around—a turnaround that continued under new leadership after Kindler left McDonald's. However, he did not abandon his General Counsel duties. In fact, for much of the time that he was running the Partner Brands at McDonald's, Kindler retained his role as General Counsel.

Amazingly, these moves, despite their brilliance, were only midcareer for Kindler. He went on through a series of Opportunist GC moves to ultimately take the helm of Pfizer, the world's largest pharmaceutical company, as Chairman and Chief Executive Officer. In our view, anyone who tracks the career of Jeff Kindler will see that he is the quintessential example of an Opportunist GC—one who created his own opportunities through adding value to the business beyond the legal department and was also quick to respond to opportunities presented. Kindler's success suggests that this is a model worth emulating.

3

Law Firm to Corporation

Risks and Rewards

"You are only as good as your last billable hour in a firm. There is no long-term equity because you are selling a service. In a company environment, everyone has a common goal. You can build something."

JAMES DALTON, *former Senior Vice President, Corporate Development, General Counsel, and Corporate Secretary, Tektronix, Inc.*

Almost all of our interviewees spent time in a law firm at some point in their careers, and many of them highlighted making the transition from a law firm to an in-house role as a very significant point in their development. Without exception, those who made the move believe it was the right one. However, most of them agreed that it was a difficult choice, requiring careful balancing of the risks and rewards, and many cautioned that it is not the right choice for everyone. In this chapter, we share their assessments, as well as our own opinions, of some of the differences between the law firm and corporate environments and the advantages and disadvantages of each.

Advantages of a Law Firm

A successful career in a law firm offers some distinct advantages that appeal to many lawyers—as with most things, there are pros and cons. We begin by looking at some of the perceived advantages of law firms.

Image

While we hear much about the generally negative public image of lawyers the American public has a fascination with them. A recent *ABA Journal* article entitled "The 25 Greatest Fictional Lawyers (Who Are Not Atticus Finch),"[1] acknowledges the continuing powerful influence of the image of Atticus Finch, the central character in the great American novel, "To Kill a Mockingbird." The article characterizes Finch as "an instrument of truth, an advocate of justice, [and] the epitome of reason" and goes on to say that "[t]o lawyers, he was the lawyer they wanted to be. To nonlawyers, he fostered the desire to become one." According to the article, the public's fascination with lawyers hasn't changed—Hollywood, television, and literature still "love lawyers." Just ask John Grisham.

Predictably, not one of the lawyers among these twenty-five fictional lawyers is a General Counsel. These popular, predominantly heroic lawyers are generally either lawyers in private practice or prosecutors. This love affair (or at least public fascination) with lawyers does not seem to extend to corporate lawyers. To the extent we see them at all, corporate lawyers seem to be portrayed as heartless, soulless protectors of the corporate interests. Think Tilda Swinton in "Michael Clayton"—a General Counsel determined to bury a scandal at all costs.

Though we make this observation about public image somewhat tongue in cheek, we think it is still true that most aspiring

1. *The 25 Greatest Fictional Lawyers (Who Are Not Atticus Finch)*, http://www.abajournal.com/magazine/article/the_25_greatest_fictional_lawyers_who_are_not_atticus_finch/.

lawyers are more likely to envision themselves in a law firm than in a corporate setting. Law students are a competitive bunch, and premier law firms continue to sit "atop the pyramid of prestige and power within the American legal profession."[2] These firms provide an environment where lawyers can do more complex, high profile, and interesting work as compared to other environments.[3] And law students continue to be conditioned to believe that the best and the brightest will find their way into these venerable institutions. As such, the law firm continues to hold great appeal for many who aspire to a career in the law. And we think it is fair to say that, for many, the law firm may still be better suited to nurture and support those aspirations.

Being the Expert and Practicing Law

Law firms continue to offer something else that is very attractive to many lawyers who enter the profession—an environment where they can specialize in an area of law and become a recognized expert. This can lead to career satisfaction as well as rewards, financial and otherwise. The nature of in-house practice is very different. For the most part, the in-house lawyer cannot afford to specialize. He or she must learn to be a generalist and acquire skills that are not purely legal in nature. In the process of acquiring the necessary skills to succeed in an in-house setting, there may well be some deterioration in the lawyer's technical

2. Robert L. Nelson, Partners with Power: The Social Transformation of the Large Law Firm 1 (1988).

3. Eli Wald, *In-House Myths*, Wisconsin Law Review 2012, 407, 424 (2012) ("The practice of law at a large law firm can be incredibly rewarding. Large law firms... [d]o complex and cutting-edge work compared with other practice settings.... [L]arge law firms benefit from elite status atop the profession and offer their lawyers prestige and professional standing. Finally large law firms offer competitive pay, traditionally at the top of the pay scale, which is increasingly attractive given the growing cost of legal education.")

legal skills, particularly if those skills are in a highly specialized area. In our work with in-house counsel, we have found that becoming comfortable with the loss of that expert status can be difficult for some lawyers and may also make it more difficult to return to a law firm if the lawyer ultimately decides that an in-house role is not a good fit. However, some of that loss may be counterbalanced by the increased access the returning law firm lawyer now has to in-house lawyers with budgets.

A related issue is that law firms are also more likely to allow lawyers to do what most lawyers prefer to do—practice law. Many lawyers appreciate being somewhat divorced from the administrative aspects of running a business. While the General Counsel will be involved in the practice of law in some sense, the role is much more complex and will include, among other things, being a corporate officer and a member of the senior management team as well as the administrative role of managing the legal department. That administrative role will include personnel management, budgeting, and other duties that many lawyers do not find appealing.

A Safer Place?

Historically, another perceived advantage of the law firm has been relative employment security and stability. Law firms have traditionally been seen as fairly stable institutions where involuntary departures of lawyers were rare generally and almost unheard of after a lawyer had become a partner. In a 2006 article discussing how he had built GE's legal team, Ben Heineman shared an anecdote about a law firm partner's expectations regarding employment security:

> One law firm partner, having agreed to join GE, called to say he had forgotten to ask one question: how long was his

> contract? My response: "One day." At this level, we were all "at-will" employees, just like all senior GE leaders. We were making a personal bet on our skills and a financial bet on the company.[4]

Of course, we know that the recession that began in 2008 changed the "security landscape" rather dramatically. Large law firms laid off associates and staff in record numbers in 2008 and 2009, and significant numbers of partners were either dismissed or demoted to nonequity status.[5] Nonetheless, even today law firms are likely to be viewed as more of a meritocracy-based environment where working hard and doing good work provides a lawyer with some assurance of job security. This is still in contrast to today's corporate environment where the possibility of getting fired is just a fact of life and may have nothing whatsoever to do with performance.

James Dalton had an early experience as a young in-house lawyer at Tektronix, Inc., then the world's leading manufacturer of specialized test and measurement instruments, where he observed the firing of a respected General Counsel following a change in CEOs. This experience brought home to him the reality of the relative instability of the corporate world. We describe this as his "tuna salad moment," for reasons that will become clear:

> When I joined the company as an in-house lawyer, my boss, Allan Leedy, was the General Counsel. Allan was an extraordinary guy—he practiced law in English, French, and German and was the acting CFO for a year. A few years later,

4. See Heineman, Ch. 1, *supra* note 15.

5. See Bernard Burk & David McGowan, *Big But Brittle: Economic Perspectives on the Future of the Law Firm in the New Economy*, 2011 Columbia Business Law Review 1, at 28–29 (2011).

> the company hired a new CEO who decides we need a culture shock to move the company where it needed to be. That meant the old guard had to go, and he brought in a new General Counsel.
>
> Shortly after the change, the new General Counsel invited me to his office for lunch. I had been asked to do an asset analysis on some of our lines of business. I remember that we were eating tuna sandwiches. He asked me how things were going with the transition and Allan's departure. I told him I thought it was a big mistake to get rid of Allan—I wanted him to know it was a bad idea in my opinion. A week later, we had lunch again, and he offered me a job in corporate development, which was a step up. When I asked him why, he said, "You write well. People who write well think well. And you defended your old boss."

Although this experience was challenging for Dalton because he liked and respected his former boss, it proved to be very valuable. He notes the following as chief among the lessons he learned: "What I came to understand was that CEOs get to pick their own General Counsel. It's not right or wrong, just the way it is. The CEO gets to choose. You have to have the CEO's trust or you won't be in on the important decisions."

Later in his career, Dalton had an opportunity to apply what he had learned in a very personal setting. When Danaher Corporation purchased Tektronix in 2007, Dalton, who had guided the company through the transaction, submitted his resignation when the incoming leadership team asked him to do so. "It was a bit earlier than I would have wanted to go," he said. "But we had a great run and, when the time comes to move on, it's the right thing to do."

A recent paper published by Heidrick and Struggles, a leading worldwide executive search firm, indicates that the average tenure of incumbent General Counsel at 6.67 years closely approximates the average tenure of CEOs at 6.3 years. Consistent with Dalton's experience, the paper also notes that changes in CEOs often lead to changes in General Counsel.[6]

It is no secret that many people who are attracted to a career in the law tend to be risk averse and, thus, more likely to crave stability than their corporate counterparts in other disciplines. For those who seek stability and security, a law firm may still provide a somewhat safer environment than the notoriously unstable corporate world.

Revenue Generator v. Overhead

Perhaps one of the principal advantages to being a lawyer in a law firm stems from being in the exalted position of revenue generator, in contrast to in-house lawyers who are viewed as part of a cost center or "overhead."

> The inherent difference regarding the role of lawyers in law firms and in-house [is this]: while at law firms, lawyers are a profit-center and the growth of the firm is desirable when financially justified; at in-house departments, lawyers are a cost-center and the growth of the legal department is generally understood as undesirable.[7]

This can have significant implications for how the General Counsel and the legal department are viewed within the corporate hierarchy, particularly if the General Counsel fails to understand and appreciate the difference. Rich Josephson, Senior Vice President,

6. Victoria Reese & Lee Hanson, *The General Counsel in 2011: A Rapidly Expanding Role*, http://www.heidrick.com/publicationsreports/Pages/default.aspx).

7. Wald, *supra* note 3, at 434.

General Counsel, and Secretary of Schnitzer Steel, a global leader in the metals recycling industry based in Portland Oregon, who joined Schnitzer in 2006 after spending more than thirty years in a law firm, commented on the importance of this recognition:

> We had our first management off-site meeting in the spring of 2006. At the end of the second day, we went around the table and talked about what we were taking away from the off-site meeting. My takeaway was that the business side makes the money and the corporate groups provide the services. Another way to say this is that it is important to understand what your role is. As a corporate service provider, you are not in charge—you are there to help build the team and support the organization. I've tried to follow that approach, and I think it has been successful.

Josephson's story displays an enlightened and ego-managed approach to assessing his new place within the corporate hierarchy. Others have undoubtedly required more time, and experienced more difficulty, in coming to a similar conclusion.

The Water Cooler

Despite the reputation law firms have for being challenging work environments, several of our interviewees acknowledged that, as lawyers in law firms, they often experienced greater potential for collegiality. This is attributable in large part to the fact law firms are much less hierarchical organizations where the lawyers' roles are basically the same and success is measured by fairly objective criteria—billable hours and new business generation, for example. The General Counsel role in the corporate enterprise is far more complex and can be isolating. Unlike in a law firm, the General Counsel often cannot share sensitive information with peers and may have no one internally to turn to for guidance in a challenging situation. In certain instances, the responsibilities of the General Counsel to the Board of Directors or other constituencies may even put him or her at odds with the CEO or other members of senior management.

Regarding the difference in collegiality, Rich Josephson observed:

> At a firm, you can be close friends with your colleagues because it's a flat organizational structure. But in a company, it's a completely different dynamic. It's all about the organization chart and where people report. There is much more potential for conflict. It is just part of the way business operates. That aspect of my move was somewhat surprising.

A More Tolerant Environment

Law firms are also viewed as more tolerant of the "quirky" (or sometimes just bad) behavior that some lawyers display. One can definitely find challenging personalities in the corporate setting, but most corporate environments place greater emphasis on collaboration or "playing well with others" and are less likely to embrace behaviors that do not conform to acceptable social norms because someone is a "genius," the preeminent expert in her field, or a top revenue generator. Also, many lawyers thrive on competition, cherish their autonomy, and may find it difficult to function in an environment where they must work collaboratively. Due to the greater emphasis placed on teamwork and leadership in the corporate setting, many lawyers coming out of law firms have had difficult times making this switch.

One of the coauthors of this book, Eva Kripalani, had some difficulty adjusting to the different expectations of a corporate environment. She had learned some very bad habits in the law firm setting. When she was working on a high intensity project, she had a tendency to become frustrated and would occasionally lose her temper with others who were not meeting her expectations. Although she is sure it did not escape notice—particularly by the victims—that kind of behavior seemed to be tolerated—even rewarded—with little or no comment about the negative impact it had on others if she was able to produce results. And the damaged relationships were of less consequence because it was fairly easy to request assignment of different associates and support staff on the next project.

When Kripalani moved to a General Counsel role, she found that certain behaviors that had served her well in a law firm setting were not productive. Her new corporate colleagues viewed the sense of urgency that had earned her a reputation within the law firm for "getting things done" less positively. At one point, the senior Human Resources executive, with whom she constantly seemed to be butting heads, called Kripalani into his office and told her that her late night emails and voicemails were not conveying a positive impression that she was a hard worker but instead conveyed the negative impression that she was not effectively managing her time. She also received feedback about her air of impatience, condescending tone of voice, and other "bad behavior." Those lessons were difficult and ongoing for a few years, but they were necessary. On a more positive note, the Human Resources colleague who was her nemesis became a friend and mentor in the process.

Choosing to Make the Move

So, given these advantages of a law firm, why did the people we interviewed choose to make the move?

For many of them, they were perfectly happy in the law firm when opportunity knocked, as was the case for Kindler, Villarreal, and Josephson. However, for most of them, they seemed to know fairly early on that the law firm wasn't the right fit for them. They expressed frustration about the limitations of an outside lawyer's role and a desire to be more involved in the businesses of the clients they represented. Still others were also concerned about the future prospects of the law firm business model. James Dalton's description of the reasons for his move touches on both of those reasons:

> I practiced in a small law firm for about three years before I decided to apply blind for an in-house position at Tektronix. I had gotten good experience and had some good client relationships but became disillusioned with the law firm early on. I could see that the demographics were going to change, and they were already starting to pull the ladder up by increasing the partnership track from five to six to seven years. Also, I always worked really hard, but I didn't like billing clients who were struggling financially. I worked twelve hours a day and billed seven. I think I may have been more pragmatic than some of my peers—more bottom-line focused on behalf of my clients.

Stephen Krull, Executive Vice President, General Counsel, and Corporate Secretary of Con-way, Inc., a publicly traded transportation and logistics company headquartered in Ann Arbor, Michigan, spent even less time in a law firm than Dalton. When he graduated from law school in the late 1980s with a degree in business, he went to work at Sidley & Austin in Chicago, where he had clerked during law school. He was doing asset securitization work, and the firm wanted him to develop a specialty in that practice area. By focusing almost exclusively in that area, he "became very good, very fast," and after less than a year, he was assuming lead roles in transactions. Unfortunately, though, he found dealing with nothing but Article 9 of the Uniform Commercial Code and the Federal Bankruptcy Code "excruciatingly routine." As he described it, "I was not an architect, just a technician. I didn't get to be involved in the 'why' the client was doing the deal, and I wanted to know that."

Part of a Real Business

Boehringer Ingelheim is one of the world's leading pharmaceutical companies. Marla Persky, its Senior Vice President, General Counsel, and Corporate Secretary, had been working as a litigation associate in a Chicago firm for only four years when she "realized that the law firm was not really an efficiency business." She decided to leave because she found herself becoming uncomfortable with tying her future to partnership in a firm where she had concerns about the ability of the partners to run a business.

Regardless of their reasons for leaving, all of our interviewees agree that life on the inside was a significant improvement for them and that the rewards were considerable. When we asked them about what aspects of the General Counsel role appealed to them, the responses were wide ranging, but all were consistent about one thing: the opportunity to learn more about the business and contribute in a more meaningful way to its success is an important advantage of an in-house role.

Peter Bragdon, Senior Vice President of Legal and Corporate Affairs, General Counsel, and Secretary of Columbia Sportswear Company, a leading innovator in the global outdoor apparel, footwear, accessories, and equipment markets, headquartered near Portland, Oregon, shared this colorful description of what he enjoys about his role:

> I am fortunate to be in a place where I can get out of the cage and be a "free range lawyer." If you asked our CEO about me,

> he would say "oh yeah, he's our lawyer," but my role is more than that. I am valued for my judgment and experience as well. Like the little fish that sticks to the shark, I go along for the ride. I have been there at the beginning of an idea, I have helped implement the idea, and on those occasions where an idea has turned out poorly, I was there to help clean up the mess, too.

Bragdon's comment illustrates an important point about a major difference between the in-house and outside counsel roles, which is the ability, as well as the need, to take more risks in the in-house role. Law firm lawyers are trained to avoid risk and, in general, to steer clients toward the lowest risk alternative. In-house lawyers must learn to be more comfortable with risk and manage it effectively within the context of the organization's overall tolerance for risk. MardiLyn Saathoff had these comments about the difference in the roles of outside counsel and in-house counsel with respect to managing risk:

> I appreciate being able to ask outside counsel to help me when I have come to a risk-based decision, and I want to know if they can support my legal conclusion. But I can't say to outside counsel "here is the problem and what should we do?" Instead, I need to ask them if the actions we propose to take are supported by my legal conclusion and are they defensible—will they be prepared to defend if necessary? We can outsource legal analysis but we cannot outsource making the risk-based decisions.

The General Counsel we interviewed seemed to embrace the opportunity to make risk-based decisions. Many of them expressed frustration that the outside counsel role had them sitting on the sidelines giving legal advice in the context of a confined set of facts presented to them without a clear understanding of the bigger picture—the goal or goals the business was trying to achieve. Many also found they had a point of view they believed to be of value to the business that did not constitute legal advice but were uncomfortable expressing it because of the limitations of their role as outside counsel.

However, it is important to recognize that the sidelines may be a more comfortable place for many lawyers, who may not adapt well to making risk-value trade-off decisions. It is also true that moving in-house will not necessarily alleviate the frustrations of those who long for an environment where their counsel is valued on more than just legal issues—particularly in the shorter term. In a recent blog post entitled, "What you are not taught at General Counsel school,"[8] London-based General Counsel Brett Farrell humorously describes the divide that can exist between expectations and reality and what it may really mean to be "more involved in the business" as an in-house lawyer:

> Working in-house comes at a cost—it's not all long lunches with private practice firms. The price you pay is career accountability where you will actually live and die by your decisions and you will be forced to make them. Your CEO or Managing Director is thinking that "you are paid enough bloody money to have an opinion, damn well give me one!"

Farrell also comments on a communication dynamic well understood by those who have served in in-house roles. "Businesspeople" often resist opinions expressed by the lawyers concerning business issues, but businesspeople do not hesitate to challenge the lawyers regarding legal advice.

8. Elizabeth Dilts, *An Online General Counsel Imagines a School for GCs*, Law.com (June 26, 2012), http://www.law.com/jsp/cc/PubArticleCC.jsp?id=1202560742986.

Amy Schulman, Executive Vice President and General Counsel of Pfizer, advises caution to the General Counsel when weighing in on business issues:

> Given the work we do in an organization, General Counsel often are involved in a number of areas. While we may be tempted to weigh in on each issue we see, finding the right balance is important. Knowing when to speak up and offer one's perspective and when to stay silent and listen to others' expertise are equally important for any General Counsel.

Social Responsibility

Another consistent theme from our interviews is that the General Counsel seat is viewed as a more effective position from which to advance socially responsible initiatives, such as diversity and inclusion and corporate pro bono programs benefiting their communities. Although many law firm lawyers also give generously of their time to promote such initiatives, General Counsel have emerged as leaders, as observed from the visible leadership roles of a number of the General Counsel we interviewed. There is no one in this group who does not deserve recognition for the significant contributions they have made to their professions and communities. We call out here just a few specific examples.

P.D. Villarreal

Villarreal is a staunch civil rights advocate and diversity champion. He has received countless awards for his work in diversity, including a 2012 "Award for Outstanding Contribution to Diversity in Alternative Dispute Resolution" from The International Institute for Conflict Prevention & Resolution (CPR Institute), recognizing him "as a proponent of diversity and, in particular, for the inclusion of African Americans, Latinos, and women in ADR for many years." For Villarreal, who is a Mexican-American born and raised in modest—if not challenged—socio-economic surroundings in San Antonio, Texas, the "fundamental message" of the diversity movement is: "[n]ot rigid categories, not quotas, not head counting, but diversity of thought, innovation, and creativity driven by diverse and multicultural teams. Diversity as a competitive advantage. Diversity as a strategy to win!"

Villarreal has spent more than two decades implementing innovative diversity initiatives at General Electric, Schering Plough, and now at GlaxoSmithKline. He founded GE's award-winning Legal Department Diversity Initiative that increased the composition of its diverse in-house lawyers by forty-three percent in just one year (2000) and he has continued to lead the charge at each of his later work places. He is also a founding board member of the Minority Corporate Counsel Association, where he has championed the hiring, retention, and promotion of diverse attorneys in legal departments and the law firms that serve them.

Marla Persky

Marla Persky has also been a leading advocate for diversity and firmly believes that it is one of Boehringer Ingelheim's competitive advantages. She has this to say about her experience with diversity: "I have personally practiced law long enough to know what it is like to be in the minority—the only woman in the room in many situations. I have worked on both diverse and nondiverse teams. The team effectiveness and work product is always better on diverse teams. In any organization, a diversity of thoughts, experience, and people creates better results."

Persky has received numerous awards and recognition for her work in diversity, including the 2012 Edwin Archer Randolph

Diversity Award from the Lawyers Collaborative for Diversity, a Connecticut-based organization dedicated to increasing diversity within the legal profession; the 2011 Corporate Leader Award from The Lesbian, Gay, Bisexual & Transgender Community Center in New York; and a 2011 Corporate Leader Award from the Connecticut Hispanic Bar Association. Persky is past president of the Lawyers Collaborative for Diversity and is also a founding member of the Leadership Council on Legal Diversity, an organization of corporate chief legal officers and law firm managing partners dedicated to creating a truly diverse legal profession.

Compensation

Interestingly, almost no one we interviewed cited compensation as a principal motivating factor for their move from a law firm to a corporate legal department. In fact, for some, the move in-house involved an initial reduction in compensation. However, it was clear from our interviews that better opportunities for advancement and compensation were factors weighing in favor of the move to a General Counsel role. A recent CorporateCounsel.net blog post summarizing the results of a 2012 study on General Counsel compensation by Equilar, a leading executive compensation data provider, supports that better compensation opportunities continue to be an important consideration in seeking a General Counsel role.[9] A number of interesting facts about General Counsel compensation are included there. The growth rate of General Counsel pay outpaced CEOs and CFOs in 2011. For the 136 General Counsel at Fortune 1000 companies who participated in both Equilar's 2012 and 2011 Top 25 Surveys, median total compensation increased 2.4 percent in 2012 compared to 2011. The 2012 increase was modest compared to the

9. See Romanek, Ch. 1, *supra* note 21.

12.8 percent increase experienced in 2011. The 2011 growth rate compares to 6.2 and 8.9 percent growth rates for compensation of S&P 500 chief executive and chief financial officers over the same time frame.

The blog post also had this to say regarding the comparison of General Counsel compensation to that of executives other than the CEO and CFO:

> The General Counsel role is replacing operational executives in importance. The number of General Counsel identified as named executive officers among the S&P 1500 index has grown from 494 individuals in 2007 to 591 individuals in 2011, a 20.9 percent increase. The importance of the legal position appears to be pushing out the operational executives from the five highest paid positions as the number of chief operating officers and vice presidents of operations have fallen by 13.3 percent, a decrease from 835 in 2007 to 724 in 2011.[10]

Billable Hours and Work-Life Balance

Rich Josephson expressed one of the more frequently noted advantages of moving in-house when he told us "the first good thing about working for the company was not keeping a timesheet. I liked dealing with the task as opposed to the use of my time." He noted that this change in orientation gives him the opportunity to take a more proactive approach to problem solving for the company:

> In a firm, it's a largely reactive position where you do the work that comes in rather than proactively identifying the

10. *Id.*

> risks by asking yourself: "What is keeping me up at night? What are we not doing that we should be doing? What do I not know that I should know?" The General Counsel role gives you the opportunity to consider those questions.

Josephson was one of many of our interviewees to express relief at being freed from the tyranny of the billable hour. However, this freedom should not necessarily be equated with an easier life as compared with working in a law firm. Many of our interviewees made the point that they work just as hard—or even harder—than they worked in a law firm and that any expectation of better work-life balance in an in-house environment may be somewhat illusory.

In a recent article, one legal scholar challenges the "failed promise of in-house practice" and characterizes as "prevailing myths" the promises of better work-life balance and gender equality of in-house environments as compared to law firms.[11] The article refers to the "infatuation of large law firms' lawyers with the notion of going 'in-house,'" noting that it is informed by the "hypercompetitive and glass ceiling realities in large law firms and a dearth of actual information about in-house practice."[12] With respect to work hours, Professor Wald posits that the in-house lawyer will likely need to spend a considerable number of "soft" hours proving his or her worth to the business and that how to spend them effectively is often unclear, which may lead to the in-house lawyers spending more, not less, time at work than in the more structured environment of a firm. He also notes that

11. See Wald, Ch. 3, *supra* note 3.

12. *Id.* at 418. He goes on to say that "[m]uch of the existing literature on in-house counsel is of little help to lawyers interested in learning more about in-house positions. To begin with the scholarship's emphasis on the increased role and prestige of in-house counsel might serve unintentionally to foster illusions of greener pastures."

the career paths to advancement are often less clear in-house and they may not even exist. To the extent those paths exist, they may require more sacrifice in terms of willingness to travel and relocate.

The bottom line is that the grass isn't necessarily greener on either side of the pasture. There are considerable challenges to be faced in both the law firm and in-house environments, and it is important to understand them when making a choice between them.

4

Transitioning from Firm to Corporation

"There is a period of adjustment when you move from a firm to a corporation. Some things are easy—they are like big bright lights—but determining how much risk to take is hard. Law firms teach you to eliminate as much risk as possible. This can create tension and challenges."

HILARY KRANE, *Vice President and General Counsel, NIKE, Inc.*

As discussed in the previous chapter, there can be many reasons behind a lawyer's decision to leave the familiarity and relative security of a law firm for the less predictable environment that awaits a General Counsel. Regardless of the factors that tip the scales in favor of making the move, the transition is likely to be challenging.

Back to School

Law schools have traditionally focused on preparing lawyers for law firm or public sector practice and have not offered courses focused on the issues in-house counsel face. This is starting to change, but very slowly. Recently, law schools have encountered more vocal criticism from clients as well as from academia for adhering to traditional curricula that fails to prepare graduates to solve real legal problems.[1] The expectation has long been that

1. See Judith Welch Wegner, *The Carnegie Foundation's Educating Lawyers: Four Questions for Bar Examiners*, The Bar Examiner, June 2011. See also, Burk & McGowan,

law school graduates would acquire the practical problem-solving skills they need in law firms while working on actual client matters. The problem is that clients have grown tired of bearing the cost of that training and are bringing pressure to bear on both law schools and law firms to find a better method of educating and training young lawyers.

Enhancing the Curriculum

While the continuing debate over practical training in law schools continues, there does seem to be some movement toward providing courses designed to prepare students for in-house careers.[2] For example, as of this writing, Columbia Law School offers a course entitled "Role of the Modern In-house Counsel." The course description reads in part as follows:

> This course examines the strategic role of the modern in-house counsel and changes in the legal and regulatory environment that underlie its new importance. We will look at the demands on the in-house lawyer of combining the roles of legal guardian and business partner, and consider the skills and capabilities needed for success. We will discuss how the prominence of in-house counsel has drawn the attention

Ch. 3, *supra* note 5, at 112–113 ("As increasing numbers of sophisticated clients refuse to pay high rates for inexperienced lawyers, the debate about new lawyers' practical preparation and who should be providing it has gotten louder and more pointed, though no clearer. The role of practical training in the future of legal education remains murky, with many new initiatives in the academy and the Bar only recently underway.")

2. See Sue Reisinger, *Law Schools Offering More Courses for In-House Careers, Corporate Counsel* (October 19, 2012), http://www.law.com/corporatecounsel/PubArticleFriendlyCC.jsp?id=1350250967651.

> of regulators, who have imposed new requirements on the position and stepped up enforcement actions and prosecutions. We will address how the different role the inside counsel serves entails ethical, privilege, and liability challenges not shared with outside lawyers. We will also consider the impact of inside counsel as today's most significant purchasers of legal services. *We will look at how in-house lawyers have revolutionized the global legal marketplace, driving disaggregation and outsourcing of legal services, requiring alternative billing, sparking the rise of Internet-based providers, and recasting the relationship between companies and their outside counsel.*[3] (emphasis added)

Another example is Harvard Law School's course entitled "Challenges of a General Counsel Seminar," which "explore[s] the three fundamental roles of lawyers—acute technician, wise counselor, and lawyer as leader—in a series of problems faced by General Counsel of multinational corporations," using case studies from contemporary real world challenges, such as the BP oil spill, Google's clash with the Chinese government, the Mark Hurd resignation from Hewlett Packard, and the News Corp hacking scandal.[4]

In addition to the recent efforts law schools are making to educate aspiring lawyers about the issues and challenges General Counsel and other in-house lawyers face, law firms and their clients also are collaborating to provide training opportunities for new graduates in a mutually beneficial way. One of the more

3. *Law School Course L6368 Role of the Modern In-House Counsel,* Columbia Law School, Offerings for 2012–13, law.columbia.edu, http://www.law.columbia.edu/courses/L6368-role-of-the-modern-in-house-counsel.

4. *Law School Seminar, Challenges of a General Counsel Seminar*, Harvard Law School, law.harvard.edu (Fall 2012), http://www.law.harvard.edu/programs/plp/pages/courses.php.

well-recognized endeavors is the "Pfizer Legal Alliance (PLA) Junior Associate Program" initiated by Amy Schulman, Executive Vice President and General Counsel of Pfizer, which is discussed in more detail in Chapter Five. One of the many benefits of the Pfizer Junior Associate Program and similar programs for new lawyer participants is helping them to make an early and educated decision about whether they are better suited to a law firm or an in-house role.

Law Firm Training

Though innovations in law school curriculum and collaborations such as Pfizer's Junior Associate Program may better prepare lawyers for an in-house role and may even alter the conventional career path to the General Counsel seat in the future, almost all General Counsel we interviewed received their legal training in law firms. Unfortunately, law firms also generally fail to provide training in the management skills that are needed in the General Counsel role.

Lawyers generally receive no exposure to management principles in law school, and few of them receive any systematic training in law firms. Lawyers who serve in management positions in firms usually do so on the basis of their work as practicing lawyers, since there is no established track within firms for attorneys who are interested in moving into positions of authority. Lawyers who coordinate the work of litigation or transactional teams also tend to be successful lawyers who have good relationships with clients rather than those who have demonstrated the ability to manage projects. The qualities that are useful in building a successful law practice are not necessarily those that make for an effective manager.[5]

5. Milton C. Regan & Palmer T. Heenan, *Supply Chains and Porous Boundaries: The Disaggregation of Legal Services*, 78 Fordham L. Rev. 2137, 2163 (2010).

The General Counsel we interviewed acknowledged the limitations of law firm training to adequately prepare them for their in-house roles. However, many also cited their law firm experience as an essential step on the path to becoming a General Counsel. This comment from Schnitzer Steel's Rich Josephson is representative: "A minimum of three to five years in a law firm is the most valuable training you can get anywhere. You learn how to work really hard. And that firm experience helps build law into your DNA, which helps you make the right decisions."

We should acknowledge that most of our interviewees spent time in law firms before "clients [were] imposing price pressure on outside law firms, and increasingly insisting that the cost of practical training be stripped out of the price they pay for the legal services they buy."[6] As a result, the legal training they received in law firms may have been of a different character than the training that has been provided in more recent years. The changes in law firm economics that began in the late 1970s and early 1980s have significantly impacted the quality of law firm training. As noted by one legal scholar:

> [P]artners were under pressure from every direction: greater numbers of associates per partner to oversee; greater pressure to bill more, but bill only time and tasks that would survive in-house counsel's or a fee auditor's scrutiny; greater misgivings from clients as associate rates soared to pay for anything resembling on-the-job training. Associates saw less and less of the experienced practitioners and firm leaders who in past generations had taught by observable example, and, in many cases, by personal tutelage as well. With smaller, more routine transactions and cases more frequently reserved for the client's own less expensive in-house legal staff, junior

6. Burk & McGowan, Ch. 3, *supra* note 5, at 115.

> associates at elite firms were more often forced to find their training (if they found it at all) as deeply subordinated members of crowded "teams" in large, complex matters.[7]

Law firms are seeking solutions to the problem of associate training and have responded in a variety of ways. These include secondments to public agencies (such as prosecutors' or public defenders' offices) or client legal departments, enhanced training programs and "apprenticeship" programs in which associates spend their first two years predominantly in training, with substantially reduced salary, minimal billable-hour requirements, and a developing curriculum of skills instruction. In addition, some firms are moving away from seniority-based associate compensation in favor of "merit"-based compensation that rewards the acquisition of skills and experience.[8]

Baptism by Fire

Despite these concerns about deterioration in the quality of law firm training, the General Counsel we interviewed generally agreed that spending time in a law firm continues to be valuable training for an aspiring General Counsel. However, there was also a shared perception that most outside lawyers have limited visibility to and understanding of the General Counsel role. As one of our General Counsel (who asked not to be identified out of respect for his outside counsel relationships) commented: "Except for the most senior of them, most law firm lawyers have a limited view of what their clients are actually doing. They are

7. *Id.* at 24–25.

8. *Id.* at 114–15.

removed from it. Their role is somewhat like that of a plumber or an electrician—they install the plumbing and the wiring, but they don't live in the house."

As a result, the learning curve following a move to an in-house position is usually a steep one. Many of the General Counsel we interviewed described their initial transition as one in which they encountered a somewhat bewildering landscape that operated far differently than the one they were accustomed to at the law firm. What we heard from them offers valuable insights into the kinds of challenges a new General Counsel is likely to face in making the transition, as well as some ideas about how to overcome those challenges.

They also offered guidance for evaluating a potential opportunity and for making any resulting transition as smooth as possible. Their advice generally fell into the following categories, upon which we will elaborate in this chapter:

- Candidly assess your personality, your skills, and your experience in determining whether the GC role will be a good fit.
- Be aware of the challenges that await you.
- Assess the company, including its culture, its track record on business integrity, and how the CEO and other senior management view the role of the General Counsel and the legal department.
- Carefully evaluate the terms of the offer and the situation to make sure you get what you need to be successful.

The Suit Won't Fit Right "Off The Rack"

Is there a one-size-fits-all list of qualities and characteristics someone needs to make a good General Counsel? Not surprisingly, the answer to that question is no. This is in part because each organization is different and its needs, culture, and leadership personalities will dictate to some extent the skill set and personality of the individual who is likely to be a success in the role. But successful General Counsel share some common characteristics.

Perhaps the most universally cited quality required for an effective General Counsel is good judgment. This essential quality is not easy to define, but it definitely involves the ability to effectively consider and evaluate different outcomes of a decision or course of action and take or recommend actions based on the conclusions reached during that process. We often hear that judgment is something that is hard to teach, but experience plays an important role. As Will Rogers famously said, "Good judgment comes from experience, and a lot of that comes from bad judgment." Before assuming a General Counsel role, it is important for an aspiring General Counsel to have had his or her judgment tested in a variety of difficult settings that demonstrate the ability to make good decisions.

NW Natural's MardiLyn Saathoff reinforced the importance of judgment in the context of her story about being hired as the General Counsel to Oregon's Governor in 2003. During the interview, the Governor asked her if she thought she was qualified for the job. She told him she believe she was a good lawyer and knew something about the role of the Governor's General Counsel, but that she was essentially an in-house business attorney and could not claim to be skilled in many of the areas for which the Governor's General Counsel was responsible. His response: "I don't really need anyone to tell me what the statutes say or what the law on a topic is, but I really need someone who has judgment. When I talk to people about what I need in this position your name keeps coming up, and it's about judgment."

Brad Thies, Senior Vice President, General Counsel and Secretary of FEI Company, a leading diversified scientific instruments company based in Hillsboro, Oregon, had these comments about the importance of judgment:

> Many years ago, I had a boss who told me that all business comes down to a single quality: judgment. I am sure he was right. In my experience, it is far more important than raw intelligence, creativity, or even strong execution skills. The good news is that some of the capabilities that form good judgment overlap those held by good lawyers. Good judgment starts with the ability to gather facts and sort the important ones from the irrelevant. It also requires a capacity to listen carefully and understand competing views. Critical reasoning is important too. Fortunately, all three of these skills can be taught and developed.
>
> Two other things that are harder to teach also figure in good judgment—an ability to accurately evaluate people and good common sense. Finally, experience is part of it too. By the way, common sense might also be thought of as an innate ability to understand and balance the risks and opportunities represented by a particular decision. Lawyers are sometimes handicapped because they overregard risk and undervalue opportunity. But if you're a good lawyer and you've got common sense and the ability to size people up, you can develop good judgment. And in business, that will be prized above all else.

The Smartest Guy in the Room?

An early lesson that proved difficult for some who made the move in-house was that their educational pedigree, prior legal career accomplishments, and important position in the organization did not automatically assure them the respect of their peers. Respect has to be earned. As Columbia Sportswear's Peter Bragdon said: "The General Counsel role is a hammer that brings you to the table—but making the most of the role, being trusted and valued, has to do with building relationships. The management team must think you can contribute to the business." Bragdon and others emphasized that by using that hammer too often or too soon, a new General Counsel will risk alienating others in the organization, which may ultimately lead to failure.

A related point is that before you can contribute to the business, you have to learn about the business or, in the words of one General Counsel, learn to "live in the house." There was clear consensus that truly understanding the business and what is important to the business is a necessary prerequisite to acceptance of the General Counsel as a valued member of the corporate leadership team. As discussed in more detail in Chapter Two and below, many of our General Counsel acquired this understanding by actually spending time in business roles, while others amassed the necessary understanding in other ways. Whatever the path, it is critical to thoroughly understand how the company makes money. As obvious as this sounds, we heard from a surprising number of people that this can be a stumbling block for lawyers because they are accustomed to acquiring knowledge about multiple client businesses using more of a "mile wide and inch deep" approach.

In addition, lawyers who are transitioning to the in-house environment often continue see their roles as focusing on the legal issues, which is where they are accustomed to adding value. However, effectively serving a business in an in-house role requires much more extensive knowledge about the company's business, including how its products and /or services are made and/or delivered, priced, marketed, and sold; the company's customers and competitors; and a variety of other things with which lawyers on the outside may not typically concern themselves.

We asked Elizabeth Large, Executive Vice President and General Counsel of Knowledge Universe-US, the nation's largest private provider of private early childhood education, how she explains to new members of her team what it means to understand the business.

> You can say the words "you need to be integrated in the business," but if you are coming from a law firm environment, that doesn't tell you anything. It may tell you that you are supposed to be doing something you are not doing, but what is it? More context is needed so they can understand what is expected of them. Of course, understanding the business requires some understanding of the company's financials and what drives revenues and expenses. It also means understanding the pain points, the risks that are inherent in the business, and the risks that the business is focused on now. But, most importantly, it means spending time where your customers are. You can read an annual report, but until you go to the front lines where your customers and employees interface, you won't understand the business. I learn something new each time I go into our centers.

Peter Bragdon agrees that understanding the business at a fairly detailed level is essential for in-house lawyers to add value:

> I don't think you can be effective if you don't understand all aspects of the business. This is a difficult concept for many lawyers, particularly those in law firms. If you operate in a global manufacturing environment, this may mean that you need to understand the mechanics of manufacturing a product in China and shipping it to Italy in order to really do your job well.

For Bragdon and his legal department colleagues at Columbia Sportswear, this has translated into focusing on customs and trade, retail, and intellectual property issues because those areas have significant financial implications for Columbia's business and, thus, are areas where the legal team can add significant value.

MetLife's James Lipscomb, whose unusual career path is detailed in Chapter Two, actually spent much of his career working his way up through the business ranks at MetLife before assuming the General Counsel role. Tektronix's James Dalton credits much of his success to the opportunity he was given to spend time in a corporate development role where he learned the business by working on corporate transactions. Tom Sabatino and Jeff Kindler both spent time moving in and out of senior leadership roles on the business side. While we heard from those who had the experience that there is no better way to learn the business than to actually spend time in a business role, other General Counsel managed to acquire their considerable business acumen while serving in the in-house counsel role or other "nonbusiness" roles.

NIKE's Hilary Krane credits her time as in-house counsel with PricewaterhouseCoopers (now PwC) for exposing her to the business issues that would prepare her for her future roles as General Counsel at both Levi Strauss and NIKE:

> At [PwC] I saw effective accounting and trusted advisor roles playing out in very crucial moments. [PwC was] close to several levels of management in businesses around the world. In crisis situations—if they were serious enough—I was involved. I saw instances where it got to a point that in-house counsel [to the business] was considered unable to handle a matter, so someone outside was brought in, but often had no deep relationship with the company. The audit team stayed there throughout—the auditor is always there. I got broader exposure to critical business issues because of where I sat.

Both Peter Bragdon and MardiLyn Saathoff credit their experience in government, as well as business, with providing them some of the skills they needed to be effective in their current roles. Bragdon and Saathoff served together on the senior executive staff for Oregon's then Governor Kulongoski during his first term beginning in 2003. Bragdon served in the Chief of Staff role and Saathoff served as both General Counsel and Business and Economic Development and Policy Advisor. Both Bragdon and Saathoff had the opportunity to acquire significant experience not only in dealing with "the snake pit of politics" but in managing people, recommending strategy, developing and managing budgets and related processes, and creating collaborative support among stakeholders to align with the Governor's agenda, among other things. These are skills that have obvious relevance in the business world and have served them well.

We have explored the career paths of many others in this book, which reflect a wide array of experiences that have allowed them to successfully execute their roles. See Chapters Two and Eight.

Building the Risk-Value Chops

Another consistent theme that emerged from our interviews is the challenge, as well as the critical importance, of learning to assess risk in a business context. Hilary Krane's statement at the opening of this chapter reinforces the point made earlier that acquiring this skill requires a significant shift from the law firm paradigm, which rewards identifying and avoiding risk. Successful corporations are those that take calculated risks and make them pay off more often than not, and a successful General Counsel must learn to assist the corporation in calculating and taking those risks.

Brad Lerman, who, at the time of our interview, was Senior Vice President and Chief Litigation Counsel at Pfizer, the world's largest research-based pharmaceutical company, had a scope of responsibilities that required him to make critical risk-assessment decisions every day. Pfizer's litigation portfolio is arguably one of the largest in the United States, if not globally. As such, Lerman faced a situation where his company was often a target rather than just a defendant. Lerman said:

> It is critical for me to provide guidance to my litigation team to balance their time between litigation avoidance and litigation response. In our environment, it is too easy to always focus on firefighting, but spending time providing guidance to the corporation on how to avoid litigation—or at least reducing the exposure in litigation—is critical to success.

This approach has clearly served Lerman well. He recently was appointed Executive Vice President, General Counsel, and Corporate Secretary of Fannie Mae.

Learning to prioritize and manage risk effectively can be one of the most difficult transitional challenges a new General Counsel will face. This is attributable to the perfectionist tendencies common among many lawyers, coupled with the training they have received in law firms. In most businesses—unlike in law firms—perfectionism is rarely considered a virtue. To put it another way, for those who aspire to do "bespoke work,"[9] the corporate legal department is probably not the right place.

9. See Susskind, Introduction, *supra* note 4.

Brad Thies talked about the importance of assessing risk in a business context, as well as how to use this ability to demonstrate value to the business:

> I recognized early that legal risk had to be put in business context. I was that type of person by the time I arrived at FEI. When I was at WebTrends, we had young, inexperienced salespeople selling software. They didn't have experience with closing a deal, and the lack of process was exposing us to significant risk. This issue surfaced very quickly. So we reset the sales process—my contribution was bringing in an experienced staff person capable of putting a process in place for closing those deals. It was an immediate hit. The COO later told me that the process drove an additional ten to twenty percent of Company revenue because it improved the efficiency of the sales force and gave them a way to bring their deals to close faster (and with reduced risk, I might add). My career has been about bringing sensible, simple processes to bear on risk in the organization.

Thies described making this change as a relatively simple "quick win" that the business could understand and appreciate.

Herding Cats

Another challenge is the pace and variety of issues to be addressed in-house, which is often a shock to lawyers who are coming from a firm. Although there is no question that law firm life can be extremely demanding, the nature of the law firm "expert" role often includes an expectation that it may take more time to produce the "right" answer. And, there is usually the added luxury of several other experts right down the hall with whom the firm lawyer can confer.

Those conditions do not exist in the typical in-house legal department where the CEO and other business leaders may wander into your office at any time and expect immediate answers to their questions. The questions rarely come neatly packaged as "legal issues," and there may not be time to do research before providing a response. For some issues, it may be important to slow things down and take more time, but, more often than not, the General Counsel is expected to have the eighty percent confidence answer off the cuff. If she doesn't, people will stop asking.

In a 2009 interview, Kim Rucker, then Senior Vice President, General Counsel, Corporate Secretary, and Chief Compliance Officer at Avon Products, Inc. (who recently became Executive Vice President, Corporate and Legal Affairs at Kraft Foods North America) commented on this dynamic in the context of the value to a General Counsel candidate of having in-house experience:

> We don't have time to do a memo to the file and check all Supreme Court precedents and then provide a "on the one hand this, and on the other hand that" approach. People want answers.... The biggest difference I see for people who have the law firm experience and the in-house experience is that ability to tell you what they think.[10]

Brad Thies offered some good "survival tips" for responding to a "fly by" question from an impatient CEO:

> I have found that managing the expectations around an uncertain answer is more important than the answer itself. Start by explaining to your [CEO] that you don't know the answer, but you will give her your best reasonable guess. Be

10. Egon Zehnder International, *Selecting the General Counsel*, 2 Experts, at 5 (2009).

> clear that it is possible you could be completely wrong. Further, tell her that if the answer to the legal question is critical to the overall decision, then it is best to wait to talk with someone who knows the answer. Be firm on this.
>
> Assuming the issue is not mission critical, you should next explain your reasoning. This has the added benefit of letting you test your own answer in front of a real live "reasonable person." Next tell her when you can get a more certain answer—usually that is just a phone call or email away. Act fast. As a group, CEOs are not known for their patience. Once you have the answer, get back to your [CEO] and tell her the outcome. If you were wrong, explain why. In my experience, if you have followed all the preceding steps, this will not be a problem. If you need to fix anything because you were wrong, assure her that you will. Then when you have fixed it, make sure to tell her so.

General Counsel are being challenged on a regular basis to lead their teams to take a reasonable and practical approach to solving problems. A principle related to the advice Thies offered is that solutions should be proportionate to the problem. The co-authors of this book have come up with a phrase to describe this and have been using it to guide the strategic advisory work we do for General Counsel and their leadership teams. This phrase, "Just Good Enough,"[11] has resulted from our observations over the years that lawyers, because of their tendency to gravitate toward the risk-averse end of the risk/cost trade-off continuum, often overengineer solutions to problems. This can lead to unnecessary delay in responding to questions and implementing solutions or, worse yet, can lead to solutions that the business does not view as value added.

11. This trademark is owned by the Sumati Group, an integrated Consulting, Investment, Advisory & Services company focused exclusively on the Legal, Compliance & Information Management market, http://sumatigroup.com/.

MardiLyn Saathoff had this to say about the "Just Good Enough" approach:

> One of the real challenges to moving in-house is understanding how much legal service is enough in [that context], particularly if you are coming from an outside law firm. The standard becomes "what is the best legal service I can provide in the most cost effective way," even if I could do more on the question, topic, project, etc. Outside counsel worry about being error free. This is a standard companies for the most part are unwilling to pay for (but may unreasonably demand at times). In-house counsel worry about bringing high value quickly with low cost and minimal legal time. This, by definition, means "don't let perfect get in the way of better." That was a tag line I learned at Danaher and one I still use to guide my work on many projects.

Nick Latrenta, former Executive Vice President and General Counsel of MetLife, acknowledged that "most of our [legal] world unfortunately is grey, not white or black. Some legal issues are easy, but for most we need to help our people find a practical solution for areas in the middle." He continued by describing the best solution approach as "one that is not overburdened by process and procedure, one that allows lawyers to calibrate in their head how bad the risk is. If it is not bad—in the grey zone—then... build a solution that matches." We think this is a decision-making framework that is actionable.

Teamwork

Operating as a member of a team is another frequently cited challenge for lawyers transitioning from a law firm. Again, though this can be a function of individual lawyer personalities, law firms generally have a reputation for fostering (or at least tolerating) an environment that promotes being the smartest person in the room over playing well with others. This is due in part to the focus on individual contribution in a law firm setting rather than the collaborative approach that is more valued in a corporate setting. Hilary Krane shared her perspective on overcoming this challenge:

> How much people listen to you depends upon how much value you add. Over time, my ability to influence improved—that's true for every new member of a team. One of the most important things you learn is when not to talk and when to say something.
>
> Not everything has to be raised. Not every idea is a good one. Learning that balance is a big part of success. If you master what the company is truly about, you will have your team focused on the right things and your advice will be delivered in a way that is responsive to the people sitting at the table.

Margaret Kirkpatrick, Senior Vice President and General Counsel of NW Natural Gas Company, shared a similar perspective:

> When you are serving as outside counsel, companies are paying you for your expertise in an area. When you become part of an executive team that isn't all other lawyers, it is a completely different dynamic. You are not the "pro" who has been brought in to offer your advice. Legal counsel is supposed to serve the business by serving as a member of the team.

Appropriately, two General Counsel from companies that know a little something about team sports drove home the importance of being a team player by using sports analogies that also illustrate the important corollary principle "it's not all about you." Peter Bragdon made this point by sharing with us a favorite *New*

York Times Magazine article about Shane Battier, who was then playing in the NBA for the Houston Rockets. In the following excerpt from that article, the Rockets' then General Manager describes Battier's style of play:

> Battier's game is a weird combination of obvious weaknesses and nearly invisible strengths. When he is on the court, his teammates get better, often a lot better, and his opponents get worse—often a lot worse. He may not grab huge numbers of rebounds, but he has an uncanny ability to improve his teammates' rebounding. He doesn't shoot much, but when he does, he takes only the most efficient shots. . . . I call him Lego. . . . When he's on the court, all the pieces start to fit together. And everything that leads to winning that you can get to through intellect instead of innate ability, Shane excels in. I'll bet he's in the hundredth percentile of every category.[12]

Bragdon describes his role and that of his legal department in a very similar way:

> Lawyers inside are in a critical position where they can be, like Battier, the "Lego" block. I don't think it is possible to easily measure success of a legal department by statistics—yes, we win and lose cases, but that is for a variety of reasons, and fees go up and down, often because of the actions of others. You can't measure us just by whether other people like us, because we do a lot of unpopular things. So, there really aren't good stats to go by, but we do make our teammates better.

12. Michael Lewis, *The No-Stats All Star,* New York Times Magazine, Feb 13, 2009, www.nytimes.com/2009/02/15/magazine/15Battier-t.html?pagewanted=all&_r=0.)

Hilary Krane chose football for the sports analogy she used to make her point about the importance of teamwork:

> We want to be trusted advisors to the business versus an enforcement arm of the company. I often describe Legal as being NIKE's offensive line in the classic form of American football. We're not the big playmakers like the wide receivers, running backs, or the quarterback; we're the people on the line who know the plays the team wants to make, and it's our job to go out there and remove obstacles so the team can make forward progress and put points on the board. It speaks to the importance of Legal being embedded in the team, since no great offense would huddle without their offensive line.

It is certainly true that individual initiative is highly valued and expected from a General Counsel. But members of the team must work well together and understand the importance of each member's contribution. So, for those who are accustomed to playing by their own rules, who have trouble in collaborative settings, who cannot tolerate a peer questioning their actions, or who have trouble questioning the actions of others, moving to an in-house role is probably not the right move.

The Truth Shall Set You Free

Equally important as a teamwork orientation is the courage to speak frankly when the situation requires it. An in-house legal team can easily get a reputation for being "the Department of No" or the "Business Prevention Unit." Though this is a reputation every legal department wants to avoid, the fact is the General Counsel and her staff will need to advise caution from time to time. The General Counsel must strike a delicate balance between appropriately enabling the business to overcome legal obstacles to achieving its objectives and becoming "an enabler" who is viewed as nothing more than a mouthpiece for the business.

In her role at PricewaterhouseCoopers, Hilary Krane had the opportunity to see the General Counsel of many of their clients in action and to learn from their successes as well as their mistakes. This unusually broad vantage point provided her with many opportunities to observe "bad" General Counsel, as she identified them, and to develop her own sense of how to navigate the difficult terrain of a General Counsel faced with saying no to the business.

> I saw several situations in which there was fraud in earnings, multiple years of restatements, where I was advising the auditors. I would become a part of the team, not to manage the legal risk of the accounting firm, but to make sure that the teams on the ground had the resources they needed to evaluate what the company and the regulators were telling them and to make sure we played our gatekeeper role as we were supposed to without taking away from the auditors who were working with them.
>
> I saw who was good and who wasn't. If you had a bad General Counsel—weak, unsophisticated, or unengaged—the situation was always worse. The weak GCs were generally there as mouthpieces for the rest of the management team and lacked the ability to go to the board or push back on the executives. Or they may have been unable to stand up to their outside law firms, who sometimes would go too far. Or sometimes they wouldn't realize they had a crisis on their hands until too late in the game.

Krane is clearly not weak, unsophisticated, or unengaged, and she knows how to stand up to the business when the situation calls for it. And she can do it with her sense of humor intact, as she demonstrated when she told us "At Levi Strauss, I always said making money is only good if you keep the money."

Tom Sabatino also commented on the challenges of striking this balance:

> [As General Counsel], when business people become too aggressive, you need to stand your ground. [At one of my former companies], we advised against doing some business deals, and one of the business people came to me and said "our competitor is doing this, why can't we?" I said "we don't look good in horizontal stripes—these deals are too risky and will be bad for the company." Ultimately, he agreed. Three months later, the competitor was indicted. This is why we try to work through these things. We need to be softer on things that aren't risky and harder on the things that are.

Look Before You Leap

Starting with the basics when considering an in-house position, it is important to make sure that the industry is a good fit and to understand the company's place within that industry, as well as the company's prospects and aspirations. It is also important to understand how decisions are made and communicated. Some people are more comfortable in an informal, entrepreneurial culture, while others prefer a more hierarchical one. How the organization is structured and reporting relationships are vital pieces of information, as is information about the background and styles of other members of senior management. These are issues any prospective executive should explore, and there are numerous sources of guidance available about how to go about conducting due diligence on a prospective employer.

Certain other issues will be of particular importance to an incoming General Counsel. The first is the company's record on and commitment to business integrity and compliance. The incoming General Counsel's role in this arena is unique and, particularly in a public company, may carry a significant amount of personal risk.

The fact that a company has had a significant challenge in the business integrity or compliance arena—or a significant legal challenge of any kind—should not rule out an opportunity. In fact, it may actually be a positive factor if management has made the appropriate commitment to change, including the hiring of a strong General Counsel to assist in fulfilling that commitment. These situations may actually provide an opportunity for a new General Counsel to quickly make a positive impact in an area that is a priority for the organization. Other situations that may present opportunities for a new General Counsel to shine include supporting strategic corporate transactions and resolution of costly litigation.

Just such a career opportunity appeared for MardiLyn Saathoff in 2005 when she returned to Tektronix as its Assistant General Counsel and Chief Compliance Officer. Saathoff had been an in-house lawyer for Tektronix for a few years before deciding to take a leave of absence to serve as General Counsel to the Governor of the State of Oregon. Just as Saathoff was ending her tenure as the Governor's General Counsel, Tektronix became the subject of an investigation by the U.S. Office of Export Enforcement and the Department of Justice into its compliance with export regulations with respect to certain sales made in Asia.

Tektronix faced the possibility of serious sanctions, including monetary penalties and restrictions on exportation of certain products. Tektronix saw the need to implement a more robust export controls and compliance function and saw Saathoff as the right person to head it up; they persuaded her to return to Tektronix in the role of Assistant General Counsel and Chief

Compliance Officer. Saathoff capitalized on this opportunity, making significant enhancements to the Tektronix program, which has served as a model for other businesses.

Peter Bragdon echoed the view that big problems can create big opportunities for an incoming General Counsel, although he did not face any such challenges when he arrived at Columbia. When asked about strategies for proving your worth to the business, he had this to say: "I would tell anyone who is thinking of doing this job to find a company that has had a compliance implosion so you can come in and clean it up. That gives you an opportunity to demonstrate to the businesspeople that you know what you're doing."

Make Sure They Support You

Our General Counsel interviewees stressed that it is also important to get a sense of how the CEO and other members of senior management view the role of General Counsel and the legal department. As we heard from our interviews, trust takes time to earn, but it is possible (and important) to glean as much information as possible before accepting a position about the potential for a good relationship by asking questions and observing attitudes. Unfortunately, in some companies, lawyers are either not respected or are viewed with distrust and, depending on the circumstances, that dynamic is one that may be very difficult to change. Taking a General Counsel position in a company where lawyers are viewed as a necessary evil will likely prove unsatisfying and may be dangerous if it results in being excluded from important decisions or being denied access to important information.

Our interviewees strongly advise other aspiring General Counsel to seek out CEOs who support the role of the General

Counsel and believe in its contribution to the company's success. Support of the CEO is more likely to ensure a seat at the table when important decisions are made.

Evaluating an Offer

It is certainly important to evaluate the compensation, benefits, and other financial terms of any offer, and a number of resources are available to assist an incoming General Counsel in doing so. If the opportunity has been approached with forethought, the compensation and financial terms reflected in an offer should not be a surprise. If the company is public, information about compensation and benefits for the company's senior executives (hopefully including the previous General Counsel's) will be available from the company's proxy statement. And whether or not that information is publicly available, discussions about compensation expectations and company benefit plans should have taken place well before receipt of an offer. Related issues to consider are whether the position includes an employment contract, any severance or change in control provisions, and issues related to indemnification and director and officer liability coverage.

It's Not Just About the Money

When faced with what appears to be an attractive offer in financial terms, however, it is important not to overlook some fundamental issues that may be critical to succeeding in a General Counsel role. It is important to understand the corporate hierarchy and where the General Counsel position reports. Though there are still General Counsel positions that do not report directly to the

CEO, that is becoming increasingly rare, particularly in public companies.[13] Being considered a member of the senior leadership team and having a seat at the table where critical corporate strategy decisions are made—which we believe to be essential to properly carrying out the General Counsel role—usually means reporting directly to the CEO.[14] As Hilary Krane said about evaluating the General Counsel position at Levi-Strauss, she would not have taken the role if she was not part of the senior leadership team.

Equally important is having the commitment of the Board of Directors to the importance of the General Counsel role and the assurance of access to the Board on issues of importance. During the interview process, it is important to gain perspective on how the CEO and other senior leaders view the role of the General Counsel and the legal department, the expectations they have for them, and what metrics they would use to measure their success and evaluate their performance. Although it may take some time to understand how these views and expectations line up with present structure and capabilities of the legal department, it is important to get some sense of this before stepping into the role. If there appears to be a demand for significant change by the new General Counsel, it is equally important to understand what resources—people, budget,and organizational support—will be made available to effect that change. There will be more on that topic in the next chapter.

13. See Rostain, Ch. 1, *supra* note 14, at 473.

14. See Simmons & Dinnage, Introduction, *supra* note 3, at 146 ("Effective reporting relationships are also critical. The general counsel must report to the board of directors or, at least, the CEO. Anything less than this will inhibit the functioning of the value-creation attributes that are vital to in-house counsel effectiveness.").

Managing Costs and Resources

One of the difficult aspects of transitioning from a law firm to a General Counsel role is the need to continually prove the value of the services you provide in your own organization. Although law firms certainly deal with clients questioning the value of their services, within the firm they are generating the revenues, a position from which it is much easier to ask for resources. In-house legal departments are not only viewed as cost centers, but it often can be more elusive than with some other cost centers to explain how the costs of legal support directly benefit the business. This is particularly true with respect to the legal department's risk mitigation function, which is preventative in nature. First, it is necessary to convince others that the legal department's actions actually prevented adverse occurrences that otherwise would have happened and then to place a value on that preventative function. This can be challenging, particularly in the context of an environment where other departments in the company are competing for limited resources. Amy Schulman commented on this dynamic during her interview:

> In-house legal teams historically have struggled with how to prove their value to the company. You have to show that less visible investments, for example in robust risk-management, add value and are justifiable even when that investment may come at the cost of foregoing investment elsewhere in the enterprise.

Long gone are the days—if they ever existed—when a General Counsel could avoid being held accountable to a budget by making the argument that legal costs—at least those related to litigation—were inherently unpredictable. For some time now, CEOs and CFOs have demanded that the legal department play by the same rules as everyone else when it comes to managing budgets and predictability of costs. During the recent economic downturn, the pressure to manage costs became even greater and General Counsel are consistently saying that controlling costs continues to be their highest priority.[15] Fortunately, as we learned from our interviews and discuss in detail later in this chapter, General Counsel are increasingly innovative in finding solutions to the problem of controlling costs.

Transitioning from a law firm to an in-house position is a multi-dimensional exercise that will likely require some major shifts in focus and ways of thinking, but none of the issues covered in this chapter are intended to dissuade anyone from considering the shift. The potential challenges also present rich new learning opportunities. In our experience, good lawyers do not typically shy away from those.

15. See Altman Weil, Inc., *2012 Altman Weil Chief Legal Officer Survey*, http://www.altmanweil.com/CLO2012/.

5

How a General Counsel Builds, Leads, and Manages a Team

"I am not the star of any show. The key to building an effective team is that you have to know your own limitations and surround yourself with people who possess strengths that you don't have."

HILARY KRANE, *Vice President and General Counsel, NIKE, Inc.*

As discussed in Chapter Four, before accepting the position, the incoming General Counsel should learn as much as possible about what resources she will have to get her job done, including information about any existing members of the legal team. But regardless of how thorough and effective the pre-employment due diligence process is, it will be a key priority for an incoming General Counsel to make an independent assessment of the "resources landscape" and make certain adjustments.

Assessing and Building the Internal Team

People are the most important resource for any leader and one of the first steps in the resource assessment process should be evaluating the existing internal team. If there is no existing team, the good news is that the new General Counsel will have an opportunity to create her own. The bad news is that, in the interim, both institutional knowledge and people to help get things done will be in short supply.

Mark Roellig, Executive Vice President and General Counsel of Mass Mutual Life Insurance Company, has written extensively on the role of General Counsel and offers excellent advice on how to conduct an assessment of an existing legal department team. He advises, among other things, that before starting the job, a new General Counsel should learn as much as he or she can about the "results, structure, skills and quality of the law department."[1] He recommends reviewing the organizational charts for the company and the legal function, as well as the biographies or resumes of all of the lawyers, as well as their performance reviews and compensation information. He advises scheduling lengthy meetings with each of the General Counsel's direct reports in the first few weeks on the job and asking the following seven questions: (1) What are you working on? (2) What are your objectives? (3) Who are the "stars" in the legal organization? (4) Are there any "people" issues in the department? (5) What can the department do better? (6) What advice do you have for me? (7) What can I do to help you? He also recommends meeting with the "stars" very quickly to get their views and ideas for improvement, as well as to help cement any continuing relationship if they are chosen to continue with the team. And, of course, he suggests soliciting feedback from the CEO and the General Counsel's new peers about the department and individuals.

Knowing Your Scope and Addressing Early Challenges

In building a team, it is critical that a General Counsel understands the full scope of her responsibilities and the varied skills and experiences required on the team. Fannie Mae's Brad Lerman

1. Mark Roellig & Gordy Curphy, How to Hit the Ground Running: A Guide to Successful Executive Onboarding (2010).

said while in his prior role as Senior Vice President and Chief Litigation Counsel at Pfizer, "my remit is so broad and my team is so big that it's almost like I need to manage like a General Counsel." Brad had all litigation, discovery, government investigations, and a few other functions in his organization, represented by hundreds of professionals and hundreds of millions of dollars of annual expenditure. In addition to lawyers, technologists and legal support professionals were on the team. This diverse group needed to coalesce around Lerman's litigation avoidance strategy, and it was up to Lerman to determine how to galvanize them as well as ensure that everybody understood their role in the process.

One of the more difficult challenges for a new General Counsel may be getting the existing team to respond appropriately to a new leader. Depending on the circumstances that led to the new General Counsel's arrival, he or she may not be welcomed with open arms. As James Dalton's anecdote in an earlier chapter illustrates, the departure of a previous General Counsel, particularly one who is well liked and respected, may have left some scars on the remaining members of the team.

One of the coauthors of this book, Eva Kripalani, has some personal experience in this arena. When she left a law firm to become General Counsel of KinderCare Learning Centers, Inc., then the nation's largest private provider of early education and child care services, the company had recently been acquired, and its corporate headquarters was being relocated from Montgomery, Alabama, to Portland, Oregon.

Kripalani was asked to spend the first few months of her new assignment in Montgomery assessing the existing team and trying to learn as much as she could about the company's legal affairs. When she arrived in Montgomery, the company had been in transition for several months and, understandably, the environment was less than hospitable to the West Coast interlopers. The former General Counsel had been invited to retain her position and relocate to Portland, but had declined the offer. However, there were other members of the legal team who potentially would be offered permanent positions in Portland or an opportunity for continued temporary employment or consulting roles in Montgomery.

Although Kripalani had been involved in a number of merger and acquisition transactions as an outside lawyer, she had limited appreciation for the human toll this kind of change can exact. She found herself facing the prospect of assessing a team under very challenging circumstances. Kripalani was definitely ill-prepared, and made some mistakes along the way. One of these mistakes was being more focused on immediate knowledge transfer than building positive relationships that could be valuable to the company in the longer term. She learned that, though it was difficult to build trust with people under the circumstances that existed there, it was important to make the effort because it is very difficult, if not impossible, to make valid assessments otherwise. Kripalani thinks it would have been beneficial to her and to the company if she had focused more on establishing positive relationships and less on extracting as much institutional knowledge as possible.

Kripalani found herself on the other side of this issue several years later when the same company was sold again and merged with a competitor. Although she would survive the merger as General Counsel of the combined companies, she experienced firsthand the anxiety of her own potential job loss, the loss of jobs by her friends and colleagues, and many other difficult organizational changes. Fortunately, her earlier experiences helped her maintain perspective and made her a more empathetic and effective leader during this second transition. Keeping people focused and motivated during times of significant change is not easy, but it is both possible and critically important.

Other challenges can arise when integrating newly hired members as part of an existing team. There may be real or perceived inequities in compensation, responsibilities, or other factors that create divisions among the new and previously existing members of the team. And, of course, there can be even greater challenges in replacing members of the team.

Margaret Kirkpatrick shared this about her early experiences in making changes to her team at NW Natural:

> In the law firm your colleagues are often your dear friends. In a hierarchical structure it's different—you have to give performance reviews and hire and fire employees. Friendship with my colleagues did not translate as well in that environment. I had never fired anyone before, and the first time I faced that issue was with someone who was not doing well but who had been here a long time. When I told her she wasn't getting a raise for the first time, she actually quit. That was the easy one—others were much tougher.

Things They Didn't Teach You in the Law Firm

As previously discussed and as Kirkpatrick's comments illustrate, law firms typically do not prepare lawyers very well for the roles of evaluating talent and managing people, skills that are essential to the success of any corporate leader, including the General Counsel. Although law firms devote considerable resources to hiring the right people, hiring decisions in law firms—particularly larger firms—are often made by a select group of people charged with that responsibility, with limited, if any, opportunity for input from many of the lawyers who will be working directly with the new hires. Assessment of performance in the law firm context tends to be heavily weighted toward billable hours and other factors that focus on performance as an individual contributor. In addition, interactions between senior lawyers and subordinates may consist of a single project or a few interactions, resulting in very limited data on which to base an evaluation. A related issue is that law firms typically collect feedback on performance from a variety of sources and then deliver the collective feedback in a format that may dilute or obscure important points intended to be conveyed by the evaluators, in part because there is no personal interaction between the individuals giving and receiving the feedback. These factors and others can lead a lawyer who has been very successful in a law firm to have relatively limited experience in the skills necessary to manage and lead a team.

In a corporate setting, each person on the legal team or any other team should be evaluated for what they bring to the team and to the corporate mission as a whole. This can be very different from the type of evaluation that occurs in law firms, which tends to focus on individual contribution. In a corporate setting, it is important to have skills and personalities that balance one another. To use another sports analogy, position players are just as essential to the department's success as home run hitters. Margaret Kirkpatrick reinforced this point with her on-the-job lessons about successful hiring:

> Initially, I went for the best lawyers I could get, judging them by law firm standards. Now I look more for temperament, the ability to fit into the culture of the organization. I look for someone who plays well with others and understands our relationship with the business.
>
> I am thirty or forty percent of the total package, and everyone else has to complement that. Knowing what you can't do and having people around you who can is an essential part of the job. I prefer to have people working for me who are a lot smarter than I am in certain areas. An executive should be a good identifier of gaps and talents and be able to lead a team. Where companies have succeeded, it is because people

> played that role and had the right members on the team. Self-knowledge is hugely important for a General Counsel or anyone else.

Tom Sabatino agrees with Kirkpatrick that legal training and experience is only part of the equation when identifying the right people. "When you interview people, you interview not just for abilities but for a fit for the culture," he said.

Of course, it can be difficult for a new General Counsel who is still feeling out the culture of an organization to interview for the right cultural fit. For that and other reasons, it is important not to "go it alone" when selecting members of the legal team. Involving other areas of the business, particularly those that will be interacting with the new member, helps to ensure not only a better cultural fit but also gives others a stake in the new member's success.

According to the General Counsel we interviewed, hiring the right people is one of the most important, rewarding, and difficult tasks any leader faces. "Hire people who are smarter than you" and "hire people who have skills that you don't" were comments we heard repeatedly. As Rich Josephson said, "you need to hire people who fill in the gaps for you." As a new General Counsel coming directly out of a law firm into a company with no existing legal team, he also commented on the tremendous value of hiring someone who had previous in-house experience:

> The law firm doesn't teach you how to manage a law department. When the word got out that I had come here, Monica Rodal, who is a terrific lawyer—she had been an associate at Stoel Rives and had worked for Tektronix—called me within a week of my getting there and asked, "are you hiring?" I responded "how soon can you be here?" She understood the way an in-house legal department works. She had supported IT and HR, which were two areas I had no particular interest in. That was a major positive development for me.

James Lipscomb made the point that the immediate needs of the corporation may dictate the hiring strategy. For instance, he once hired many law school graduates and trained them in "the MetLife way." But as the company's needs changed, he made more lateral hires from law firms and other corporations. "When the company started to be more interested in the bottom line, preparing for an IPO, we would only hire the experienced lawyers we needed so there would be less training involved. We wanted people who could hit the ground running."

It takes a special recruiting talent to attract the people you want to join you in a difficult situation, either organizationally or geographically. Conway's Stephen Krull found that he could overcome a candidate's reluctance to relocate to the Rust Belt with the right pitch:

> I look for people who have faced challenges and met with success and people who love their jobs. What I sell is that you are going to love working here and being part of this team. We will work together, we will deliver great results, and we will have a lot of fun together. If I have my family with me and my health, I can live and work anywhere. For people who [have similar values], I am a pretty good salesperson.

Follow the Leader

Once the team has been assembled, the equally challenging task of leading that team begins. Many of our interviewees told us that leadership skills were not something they had learned in law school or from their law firm experience. Yet, as we listened to their stories, some very skilled leaders emerged.

As detailed in Chapter Two, before Tom Sabatino ascended to the position of Executive Vice President and General Counsel for Global Law and Public Affairs at Schering-Plough in 2004, he had successfully led the corporate legal department at Baxter International for many years. He described to us how he addressed some of the leadership challenges there, including the perceptions that there were not clear career paths for lawyers and a system for determining promotions that was not well understood.

> Schering was somewhat siloed when I arrived there. It soon became clear to me that the management of the legal department didn't know the other people in the same office. I told them that it was their job to get to know them. We did a department-wide talent review—not from a performance perspective but from a capability and ability to move up perspective. Every member of the management team had to make a presentation about his or her group. That first meeting was very frustrating for a lot of people because it forced them to talk about one another and their people, something to which they were not accustomed.
>
> We did some other important things. First, we created professional pathways—or career ladders—for all attorneys at all levels in each group that set out a grid of business, professional, and personal competencies that had to be achieved in order to move to the next level. Second, we instituted a practice that no one could be promoted without the management team discussing it first. The other thing we did was move the high talent people around to give them an opportunity to work at multiple locations. They loved it because they were able to learn new things and learn more about the organization.

We asked Sabatino whether the leadership skills he demonstrated could be learned. He responded that many things can be learned but also acknowledged the important role that personality plays:

> I think many personality types can be effective leaders, but there are some common traits. You have got to be willing to listen and learn—not talk—and you have to be able to respect the opinions of others while making clear the direction you want to go. It is important not to impose your will too soon.
>
> This does not work for the "aren't I great" personality types—lawyers who always want to tell you how smart they are. They prefer the "command and control" strategy, which will not work. You have to make sure people know where you want them to go, and then they have to have enough autonomy and authority to get the job done.

Sabatino also stressed the importance of modeling good behavior—leading by example—as well as encouraging people to "walk around and talk to each other." And he emphasized his commitment to diversity, for both his internal team and outside counsel:

> First, it's the right thing to do. But, more importantly, if you have a bunch of people who are of the same mind sitting around talking about issues, you will get one view. If you have people from different perspectives and different life experiences—women and attorneys of color—you will get a much more robust and fulsome discussion of issues.

Sabatino's observations about leadership resonated as consistent with lessons Kripalani learned in transitioning to the role of General Counsel. One of her early mistakes as a new General Counsel was adopting a "command and control strategy." As a young law firm associate, Kripalani had received feedback that she seemed reticent to take charge and was "too nice." Determined to succeed, she responded to that feedback with what she has come to see as an overcorrection. Kripalani soon developed a reputation for a willingness to take charge and for getting things done. Unfortunately, her reputation also included being very hard on subordinates, which did not seem to impede her success in the law firm environment. Because it had been successful for her, she employed the same strategy when she assumed a General Counsel role, and it seemed to work for her for a time—until it quite clearly did not. Two or three years into the role, the wheels began to come off of the bus. Although Kripalani had fairly good relationships with some of her employees—those I viewed as the "top performers"—she had poor relationships with others and soon found herself facing both active and passive resistance from some members of the team as well as complaints to the Human Resources Department.

Kripalani soon learned that, unlike in the law firm, the complaints voiced about her management style were viewed as a serious issue. She is not proud of her initial reaction to that news, which can be summed up as a combination of anger and incredulity. Fortunately, the company was willing to invest in her by sending her to a highly regarded leadership development program to assist her in learning how to address the issues she faced with her team. Many years later, her experience in that program remains one of the most challenging and rewarding of her career. Even more challenging was returning to face her team and everyone else—it was no secret that she had been sent to "charm school" (as some of her colleagues referred to it). Kripalani was embarrassed at her "failure" and still stinging from certain aspects of the anonymous 360-degree feedback solicited from her colleagues in advance and revealed to her during the program. But she had decided to embrace what she had learned and, shortly after returning, called a meeting of her team at which she apologized for her behavior and shared with them some of the ways in which she intended to address the issues that had been raised.

The response of the team was tremendous. Kripalani heard from many of them that her willingness to admit her mistakes and consider their input was much more effective in earning their respect than the command and control strategy she had previously employed. Although not always perfect, her relationships with members of her team significantly improved, as did the perception of our effectiveness in the organization.

Stephen Krull shared a story about leadership from his career that reinforces how taking risks and making mistakes can be part of developing into a great General Counsel. Krull had been at Owens Corning for a few years when the company experienced a wave of injury claims related to the use of asbestos as a fireproofing agent, which eventually led to a Chapter 11 bankruptcy filing by the company in 2000. Krull had been serving as division counsel for the roofing and asphalt segment of the business but was asked to step up and assume the role of Vice President and General Counsel of Operations so that Owens Corning's General Counsel could focus more attention on the litigation. One of his first challenges was leading a tenured team of division counsel who were still reporting to the General Counsel. He described this as his "first real leadership experience." With regard to that challenge, he said: "You can't always hire your way to a great team. In that case, I had to engage and inspire people to believe in the future of the company—so engagement and quality became my focus."

In 2002, following the bankruptcy filing, the CEO asked Krull to assume an additional responsibility as Vice President of Communications. This was at a time when, as Krull describes it, Owens Corning was receiving a great deal of bad publicity, the company's prospects were uncertain and employee engagement was at an all-time low. In addition, Krull had no communications experience and had never led a team outside his area of expertise. He was selected because the CEO believed the company needed a spokesperson who understood the legal issues the company faced and who could communicate accurate information in a reassuring way.

Krull described the experience as important to his development in at least two ways. First, it was through this experience that he learned to lead by objective setting. Because he lacked experience leading this team, he met with senior management to find out what was needed from the communications group. He then communicated that information to his team—the people who could actually deliver what was needed—and worked with them to set appropriate objectives, while also offering his support in helping them execute.

Perhaps even more significant, this experience also gave him the opportunity to make one of the most important mistakes of his career. Krull, who by his own admission was ill-prepared to deal directly with the media, was contacted by a reporter from Forbes who asked him to explain a bankruptcy-related proceeding initiated by Owens Corning to seek recovery of dividends from its shareholders. The reporter's contact occurred shortly before a meeting of the Owens Corning board at which Krull was scheduled to present for the first time. Krull described the reporter's questioning as "starting out somewhat hostile," but he believed that, by the end of their conversation, he had converted her to "a friend" and thought that she understood the company's strategy as he had outlined it. Shortly after his conversation with the reporter and shortly before Krull's scheduled presentation to the board, the article was published. Unfortunately, the reporter did not represent his comments as he had intended, and the article did not reflect positively on the company.

Krull told us he was convinced that this misstep would cost him his job. However, to his surprise and immense relief, the CEO and the board of directors supported him. The result of this experience: he received media training and moved on, having learned valuable lessons that have served him well in his career. The more obvious lesson he learned is that it is wise to keep your guard up with the media, but there was a more important lesson: you can recover from your mistakes and people will support you, especially when you have taken the time to build relationships.

We have had the opportunity to interact with subordinates of both Sabatino and Krull in other contexts and it is clear to us—and not surprising—that their leadership styles inspire the loyalty and admiration of those they lead.

Where Does the Money Go?

Never more true than in today's climate, the General Counsel must learn to lead and manage within the confines of a budget. In some organizations, simply finding out where the money is being spent may be a challenge. Margaret Kirkpatrick shared with us the difficulty she had determining the total amount of legal spend after she took the job as General Counsel at NW Natural Gas Company: "When I got here, the legal budget was all over the company," she recalls. "In different parts of the company, managers were hiring their own outside lawyers, but the legal department received all the bills. It was quite amazing."

This challenge regarding outside counsel fees was indicative of a larger challenge that confronted Kirkpatrick. The in-house lawyers were situated in different areas of the company, so, while she was charged with responsibility for managing all the legal fees, she had management responsibility for only some of the in-house lawyers the company employed. This led to Kirkpatrick's decision to centralize the legal function, which enabled her to exert much better control over both internal and external legal costs.

NW Natural is a relatively small company with only a few lines of business and only a few geographic locations, which makes centralizing the legal function much easier than it may be in a larger company that has multiple lines of business and locations. Also, the question of whether to centralize or decentralize legal services is not just an issue of providing the General Counsel with better visibility to legal costs. There are other potential advantages of centralizing legal services, such as better communication and best practices sharing among the lawyers leading to better consistency and quality in the legal services provided to the company. A centralized structure also gives the General Counsel more control. However, there are also advantages to a decentralized structure where individual business units have their own lawyers reporting to the head of the business unit. One clear advantage of a decentralized structure is that it may enable lawyers to more quickly learn and become integrated in the business.

There is no simple solution to effectively balancing these considerations that factor into selecting the right organizational structure. The right structure will depend on the individual organization and how best to serve the needs of the business. The General Counsel we interviewed came from companies representing a variety of organizational structures. This is consistent with the findings of a recent study by Oxford Said Business School Professor, Mari Sako, entitled "General Counsel with Power," in which Professor Sako interviewed fifty-two General Counsel in the United Kingdom and the United States between May 2010 and January 2011.[2] Professor Sako concluded that the internal legal departments in the companies represented typically mirror the corporate structure and is influenced by the complexity of the business and whether the company has an international presence.

2. Mari Sako & Richard Susskind, *General Counsel with Power?, Said Business School*, Oxford University, sbs.ox.ac.uk (2011), http://www.sbs.ox.ac.uk/centres/professionalservices/Documents/Sako%20GC%20with%20Power%20Aug%202011.P.D.f.

What *Should* We Be Doing and Who Should Be Doing It?

Another innovation General Counsel employ to increase efficiency and control cost involves being more strategic about determining where and how the legal department will add value. Successful General Counsel are taking a much more careful look at what the legal department is doing, who is doing it, and whether there are more efficient ways to get it done. This analysis impacts choices about internal staffing and organization structure, as well as decisions about outsourcing and technology spend, among other things.

Marla Persky asks the following questions when she is looking at whether and how the legal department should support a business process: does the legal department need to be involved at all? If so, does the legal department support require lawyers versus paralegals or other non-lawyer staff to do the work? If the process requires lawyer involvement, should the work be done in-house or should it be outsourced? She said, in her view, everything is a process and that eighty percent of what legal departments do is repetitive. She believes that the in-house lawyers should be doing the strategic work—the work that adds the most value—and should outsource the rest. She used legal department support of the purchasing function as an example. Because purchasing on the buy side is nonstrategic for Boehringer, the legal department's role is to develop purchasing contract templates for the purchasing department to use. If issues come up during the contracting process that require additional legal involvement, the work is outsourced to a law firm that has been selected to provide that support on a fixed fee basis.

This approach to allocating strategic versus nonstrategic work to in-house lawyers undoubtedly increases their career satisfaction and makes them more useful to the business. Persky acknowledges that this approach also requires a significant investment in training of in-house lawyers:

> They must be encouraged to attend meetings so they can be there to see the business people brainstorm ideas. I tell them "don't just show up for the legal discussion part of the agenda—don't parachute in and out." Being involved in the business discussions is how they will learn. The business needs to take advantage of the fact that we are not paying them by the hour.

Another innovation the General Counsel employs relates to the hiring and training of new lawyers. While still uncommon, a few companies hire lawyers directly out of law school and train them early in their careers in the unique skills of the in-house counselor. One example of a company using this strategy is Pfizer. In connection with the Pfizer Legal Alliance (PLA), Pfizer developed its PLA Junior Associate Program. Under this program, Pfizer hired three 2011 law school graduates for a two year Junior Associate Program. Each associate completes a six-month rotation at Pfizer and a six-month rotation at a firm that works closely with Pfizer through the PLA. These six-month rotations are repeated the following year. Pfizer pays these lawyers for the program's duration. At the end of the two years, the junior associates can choose whether to work at Pfizer or at the firm. Regardless of the choice, Pfizer and the firms view this as a "win-win" because the associates will have had the opportunity to learn Pfizer's business and will have established connections with both Pfizer and the law firm.

When we asked Schulman about this program, she said:

> The PLA Junior Associate Program was born of my commitment to talent development. One sign of a great in-house

legal department is the ability to train the next generation of lawyers. This program recognizes that the in-house role is unique, and we can train specifically for those roles in-house rather than relying on law firms to train for law firm-specific skills.

Bringing the Outside... Inside

There is another very important part of the team General Counsel must build and learn to manage—outside counsel. Not surprisingly, our conversations with General Counsel revealed that there are often tensions in this important relationship. They also revealed that changes in the legal marketplace have altered the dynamics and made this an increasingly challenging aspect of the job.

Members of the in-house counsel bar have long complained about the costs, efficiency, and responsiveness of outside counsel—none of this is new. However, the 2008 financial crisis and the economic downturn that followed have highlighted these tensions in relationships as General Counsel has continually been asked to do more with less. Although improvements in the economy may be providing some relief as General Counsel are beginning to report increases in their budgets and increased spending on outside counsel, considerable evidence shows that the dynamics of the relationship will continue to change.

Professor Sako's 2011 study "General Counsel with Power"[3] examined these issues in the context of the forces of globalization, digital technology, and multi-disciplinary professional knowledge, looking at the opportunities and challenges these forces present for the legal profession. She noted two major

3. Id.

agents of change: the first being the greater power conferred on in-house counsel as a result of the buyer's market created during the economic downturn and the second being the impact of new "nontraditional" entrants into the legal services market, such as legal process outsourcing providers delivering legal support services from lower cost locations. One area of focus in her study is what she refers to as "the changing nature of relationships with law firms" where she explores the use of convergence, panels, online bidding, and legal networks as tools General Counsel use in managing these relationships. One of her conclusions is that "in-house lawyers have found it challenging to provide carrots and sticks for law firms to find new ways of doing their work differently and more cost effectively."

During our interviews, we heard frequent expressions of frustration about the resistance of law firms to adapt their business models to address client needs and general dissatisfaction about law firm/client relationships. Knowledge Universe's Elizabeth Large told us that, for the most part, she thinks the criticisms of law firms are fair. "Law firms want—and they should want—those long and deep-rooted relationships that make you not want to put work out to bid, but they don't actually take many of the steps necessary to make that happen."

The sentiments Large and others expressed were consistent with results of recent industry surveys, which reveal that while law firms understand that clients' expectations about service delivery have changed fairly dramatically, they are making only modest efforts to adapt to those changing expectations and tend to focus on the potential difficulties associated with change rather than the opportunities it presents. The same surveys also reveal that clients have very low expectations of how serious law firms are about making changes. As summed up in a statement contained in Altman Weil's 2012 "Law Firms in Transition"

Survey: "Despite broad agreement that a new set of competitive trends has taken root, most law firms haven't done everything they can to change or provide greater value—and their clients know it."[4]

One unsurprising theme that emerged from our interviews was that the companies representing the largest consumers of legal services have had much more success in getting their law firms to adapt. One example is the Pfizer Legal Alliance (PLA), which Amy Schulman created in 2009 as an alternative to the traditional relationship between a corporate client and its law firms. Schulman believes that billing by the hour for legal services creates incentives that can be harmful to client–firm relationships and also may negatively affect the quality of legal outcomes. "The PLA rejects the idea of a relationship between hourly billing and value," she says.

Under the PLA, each of fifteen participating firms works on an annual flat-fee basis established at the beginning of each calendar year. The firms provide legal services to Pfizer on the full range of legal matters. The PLA handles approximately seventy percent of Pfizer's outside legal work. Firms in the PLA also are strongly encouraged to collaborate on substantive matters and PLA initiatives such as pro bono services and knowledge management. With Pfizer's assistance, the firms retool and rethink delivery of services. The firms are rewarded with opportunities to expand their scope of work on high-profile projects and to develop trust and long-term relationships with Pfizer and each other, while deepening their knowledge of Pfizer and the pharmaceutical industry.

Schulman states that the economic model of the PLA has challenged the member firms to rethink how they deliver services

4. See Altman Weil, Inc., *Altman and Weil Law Firms in Transition 2012 Survey* (2012), http://www.altmanweil.com/LFiT2012//.

to remain profitable in the new model. The firms, with Pfizer's encouragement and partnership, have introduced innovative staffing and project management approaches to manage legal work within the flat fee. Pfizer lawyers, likewise, take an active partnering role with their outside counsel to ensure effective and efficient legal support.

Now, just like any leading-edge initiative, it is important to iterate often once the initiative is implemented, incorporating feedback and real learning back into the process. Schulman acknowledges that the PLA challenged her firms to rethink how they delivered services—so much so that many of them sat in her office in the early days and complained that they "couldn't make money" in this new model. Of course, Schulman took this feedback to heart, iterated and further optimized the program so that it is yielding the business benefits that were envisioned.

Brad Lerman, who served under Schulman as Pfizer's Senior Vice President and Chief Litigation Counsel, shed some light on the give and take that was required to make this program work more effectively for both sides:

> As the largest consumer of outside counsel resources, we need to constantly be thinking about how the new flat-rate system needs to be incorporated into our daily work. How does this impact our internal team dynamics? How do we need to think of work differently? In fact, our team includes key members of our outside counsel firms and, due to the PLA operating principles, we treat them as though they are Pfizer colleagues.

It is not just General Counsel of pharmaceutical giants who are finding ways to extract more efficiency and value from the services provided by their law firms. This is an area where law firm experience can be extremely beneficial. Rich Josephson had this comment:

> One of the benefits of coming out of the firm is you know how they work and you have a better insight into how to manage them. One of the things I insist on is a relatively small number of firms. I also look for consistency in the teams [and approach]. For example, for our M&A work, one of our outside firms developed a standard set of documents. We have three different firms around the country that do M&A for us depending upon where the deals are. They now all use this standard set of documents. We have been able to maintain a small legal department in part because of our efforts to ensure that consistency.

Though some companies are pressuring law firms to discount their rates and/or offer fixed fee or other alternative fee arrangements to make costs more predictable, Josephson believes his approach has allowed him to gain better control while still using hourly billing. He said "firms ask about different billing arrangements and so on and I tell them that's the marginal stuff. What is important to me is having a competent team of people who know the company and who have local relationships."

One of the strategies NW Natural's MardiLyn Saathoff employs is to ensure that "the right lawyers are doing the right work," with an effort to have the work done by in-house lawyers where possible and to carefully frame the advice she seeks from outside counsel.

> We still go to the heavy hitter in certain cases where the risks are so high that we have to have the best. But it's not just one person or one firm these days the way it once was. We should be managing our costs by asking whether we need to use outside counsel and, if so, what kind of outside expertise

> do we really need? I tell our in-house lawyers that they add value by managing the risk without going to outside counsel. Outside legal costs are hard to manage. If I know that eighty percent of the work can be handled in-house, I can build a solid budget.
>
> When you move in-house and you are paying the bill, you suddenly get it. In-house lawyers have to be results driven. Outside counsel is not being held accountable to shareholders. They don't have the same incentive to stay within the budget.

Elizabeth Large uses a variety of strategies to manage outside counsel relationships, but she emphasizes the importance of helping outside lawyers understand the business. One of the tools she uses to increase that understanding while also building relationships is an outside counsel summit to which she invites the company's litigation counsel every other year. She characterizes it as "primarily a business update" where she and other business leaders, including the CEO and CFO, educate the outside counsel attendees about the business and update them on issues of current importance. "When we give them this information, they are fascinated by it and want more. Many of them fly across the country to Portland, Oregon, to attend. They do this all on their own nickel. We feed them—that's it."

She also offers attendees an opportunity to educate her internal team and other outside counsel about legal developments and other issues of common interest. She considers this to be time well spent on both sides and offers this advice to outside counsel about providing such educational opportunities: "Here is some low hanging fruit for client development. Don't take us to ball games. Educate us and make us smarter, but you need to understand what is important to us to make that valuable. Investing that time can be a great relationship builder."

The Other Side of the Story

In part to get a more balanced view on relationships between clients and outside counsel, we spoke to someone who has spent almost his entire career serving clients as outside counsel. Henry Hewitt is currently Senior Counsel and was a partner from 1975 through 2011 at Stoel Rives LLP. He served as chair of Stoel Rives from 1989 to 1999 and again from 2002 to 2005 and led the firm's Business Services Practice Group from 2005 to 2009. During his career, he has been the principal legal advisor to the boards of directors of some of the Northwest's most successful companies, including Tektronix, PacifiCorp, Fred Meyer, Electro Scientific Industries, and Sequent Computer Systems, in addition to many other public and privately-owned companies. He is widely acknowledged as one of the region's best and most business-savvy lawyers. His business acumen earned him a tour of duty as Executive Vice President, Finance and Administration, for PacifiCorp, then a large investor-owned utility that was later acquired by Mid-American Energy Holdings Company.

Hewitt acknowledged that the practice of law has changed significantly over the many years he has been serving clients. However, he maintains that one very important thing has not changed: effectively serving clients requires collaboration between in-house and outside counsel. Hewitt acknowledges that there has been deterioration in the relationship: "The world has suffered because inside lawyers and outside lawyers are no longer working together." He acknowledges that part of the problem is that the increasingly fast-paced environment in which today's General Counsel operate coupled with competing demands on their time, which can make it difficult to effectively collaborate with outside counsel. Nonetheless, he laments that some General Counsel seem to have lost sight of the key role that outside counsel can play in supporting them—particularly in difficult situations.

> The best relationship exists when outside counsel is viewed as a trusted advisor to the General Counsel, as well as to the CEO and the Board. There are certain things a General Counsel may not be able to say to the CEO and the Board. This is where outside counsel, in a trusted advisor role, can really add value by providing truly independent advice.

Hewitt also said that he viewed his role as that of a strategic partner with General Counsel and aspired to "help the General Counsel to be exceptional." He noted that, to the extent the General Counsel is being pressured to "do it all himself," CEOs and Boards need to understand that "if you leave it exclusively to either the inside or outside lawyers, they will get it wrong."

We think that the General Counsel we interviewed would acknowledge the importance of a close and trusted relationship with outside counsel. In fact, we view many of the initiatives they have undertaken to better manage outside counsel to be focused as much on building better relationships as they are on managing costs. In those conversations, we repeatedly heard comments about the need to align incentives on both sides. The incentives are not just economic—relationships matter.

6

Moving from General Counsel to Generalist Counsel

"The General Counsel's position in the top levels of the corporation's management structure gives the General Counsel a broad impact on strategic business planning. This may often affect the style of lawyering that a General Counsel brings to the table. Indeed top-notch General Counsel are true generalists—even renaissance persons."[1]

At some point in the career of a successful General Counsel, the hard work of acquiring the necessary skills and earning the respect of business colleagues is rewarded. We heard this achievement described in similar terms, often using the term "trusted advisor" to describe the coveted status they had achieved. Others referred to becoming "much more than a lawyer." They consistently described several common elements that brought them there: understanding the business and its objectives, learning how to communicate effectively, building relationships, establishing credibility, demonstrating leadership, and proving their ability to provide a point of view that is uniquely valuable to the company.

Understanding the Business

We heard clear consensus that truly understanding the business and what is important to the business is a necessary prerequisite

1. *Indispensable Counsel,* Introduction, *supra* note 1, at 40.

to acceptance of the General Counsel as an essential member of the corporate leadership team. As we discussed in Chapter Four, many General Counsel we interviewed acquired this understanding by actually spending time in business roles, while others amassed the necessary business acumen by supporting the business in their roles as in-house counsel.

Marla Persky shared this view about what it means to understand the business:

> A General Counsel needs to combine an external view of the business with an internal view. The internal view includes knowledge of the personality of the company, the product, the product's lifecycle and the politics, how revenue is maximized, and enough about financial accounting to spot the issues. The external view includes knowledge of the market and the industry in which the company operates, regulations affecting the company, as well as the overall macroeconomic and political environment affecting company.

As noted previously, Persky's view directly influences how she trains the lawyers who come to work for her. When she faces resistance to having lawyers attend more than just the "legal" portion of a meeting—which may come from both the lawyers and the "businesspeople"—she points out that listening to the discussions about the business reasons for pursuing an initiative or making another business decision is the best way—perhaps the only way—for the lawyers to really learn the business.

Peter Bragdon shares Persky's view that understanding the business at a fairly detailed level is essential for in-house lawyers to add value. As noted earlier, for Bragdon and his legal department colleagues at Columbia Sportswear, focusing on what is important to the business has translated into more emphasis on customs and trade issues because those are areas where the legal team can add significant value to Columbia's business. "People here from the CEO down understand the value the customs people can bring." Bragdon also used what he learned about customs to demonstrate that he knows a thing or two about leadership: "The director of customs used to report up through four layers [of management]. I spent some time with him and learned that his ideas were getting squashed by other people—they weren't bubbling up. Now that he reports to me, we can go straight to the CFO and say there is this opportunity here. We elevated him and gave him some opportunity." He is quick to add that the success of his team in adding value is "the result of a combination of the customs and trade director's talent and the role the legal department has been allowed to play at Columbia, enabling us to facilitate strategic connections." He also said "I wish I could take the credit, but for me it is good fortune."

Like Persky, Bragdon also understands the importance of training and investing in the lawyers who work for them to help them understand the business. "When the lawyers come on board I want them to go on factory audits. It's taking that time and investing in people." He laments that very few of his outside counsel seem to understand that principle but had enthusiastic praise for one lawyer from an outside firm, who "gets it." This lawyer, who has been helping Columbia with some high profile intellectual property litigation, offered to go to visit a factory in Europe at his own expense to "get to know Columbia better." He later offered to make a similar trip to China. Bragdon was clearly impressed.

Effective Communication

Almost without exception, the General Counsel we interviewed spoke of communication challenges as one of the significant obstacles they faced on their paths to becoming successful. In part, this is because legal training involves its own unique vocabulary. Though this is true of other disciplines represented in business, there seems to be something about "lawyer-speak" that seems uniquely well-suited to promoting a negative reaction among the nonlawyers in the room. We heard that the sooner a lawyer can lose that "accent," the more effectively he or she will be able to communicate in a business setting.

In a recent series of articles and related commentary regarding creating a prescribed curriculum for General Counsel,[2] communication skills seemed to be at the top of everyone's list as one of the most important subjects to be included. The comments there—as well as those we heard in our interviews—reflect a consensus that legal writing and communication, as currently found in law school curricula, does little to prepare the in-house lawyer who aspires to be a General Counsel for communicating effectively in business. To communicate effectively, lawyers must be able to get their point across in plain, clear, and concise language. As Marla Persky said, "If you can't make your point in a way your spouse or parents would understand, you probably aren't explaining it effectively—and, of course, you must never use Latin."

Hilary Krane stressed the importance of listening as an element of effective communication: "Effective communication involves understanding the needs of the people you are representing. To be a trusted advisor, you have to take your technical background and bring it to bear on the issues that are of concern to the business. In order to do that, you have to listen."

Another important aspect of communication is speaking the same language. Several of our interviewees stressed the need to understand and use the language of business—not legal terminology—when discussing an issue. James Dalton

2. See Dilts, Ch. 3, *supra* note 8.

emphasized the importance of understanding and speaking what he termed the "real language of business"—financial accounting—and the value of his early experience working in corporate development at Tektronix:

> I learned a lot from working with investment bankers on transactions. I learned that financial accounting is what drives the deals because that is how investors perceive value. Today, if you want to be a General Counsel or other senior executive, you have to understand financial accounting—it is the language of business and you can't be part of decision-making process without this understanding. If you understand financial accounting and disclosure, you can hold your own with the CFO.

Brad Thies offered a similar view:

> There is probably good reason, beyond the clichés of shared tedium, that lawyers and accountants get grouped together. In the corporate world, nearly every major legal decision or transaction has some accounting impact. And if you fail to appreciate that at some point you will end up with a disappointed CEO or CFO, no matter how brilliant your legal work. And by accounting, I don't mean just things like revenue recognition and contingent liabilities, though those are very important. Accounting issues are broader and deeper than those. In-house counsel needs to be hand-and-glove with the accounting team. Better still is the lawyer who knows enough accounting to be able to suggest creative alternatives in structuring a deal. In that way, lawyers can drive value (so long as they make suggestions humbly so as not to cause resentment among the accountants and they don't get upset if their ideas are rejected as unworkable). And don't forget about tax. You have to [be able] to talk to the tax group, too.

Thies's comments inspired a quick trip down memory lane for Kripalani, who worked in an office right down the hall from him when they were both young associates at the Stoel Rives firm. They had a common mentor, Henry Hewitt, who was known for, among other things, drilling into the minds of young business lawyers that they should live by the acronym "CATS," which was shorthand for corporate, accounting, tax, and securities. CATS provided a framework for analyzing the potential implications for every any proposed business transaction. It was very good advice that laid the foundation for thinking about things more broadly than in a purely legal context. Thies shared with us that he has carried this framework with him throughout his career, later modifying it to "CAATSIP" to include antitrust and intellectual property in the mix, reflecting his experience in the technology sector.

Establishing Credibility

Credibility is critical to the success of any General Counsel. Key foundational elements for establishing credibility include understanding the business and being able to communicate effectively, both discussed above. But, as we heard from our successful General Counsel, establishing credibility requires much more.

Credibility depends to a great extent on finding ways to legally implement desired initiatives as well as having the courage, when appropriate, to say no. By now, it seems fairly obvious that the lawyer who can do nothing more than identify the risks with a proposed course of action is going to have great difficulty establishing credibility. However, so will the lawyer who simply rubber-stamps every idea presented without appropriately identifying the risks and offering thoughtful potential solutions to address them.

Nicholas Latrenta, former Executive Vice President and General Counsel of MetLife, is an example of a General Counsel who has learned to traverse that difficult terrain very well. Latrenta spent many years on the business side as well as in the legal department before ascending to the position of General Counsel. His business experience certainly helped him establish his credibility, but it was also his willingness to challenge the business when he believed it was appropriate to do so. Latrenta had this to say about the importance of having a clear understanding of the lawyer's role:

> When a lawyer is participating in a business discussion, oftentimes a point of tension arises in that, while the lawyer can opine on the merits of the business proposition, the lawyer is always the lawyer, too. You have authority and responsibility to participate in business development, but as the lawyer, you are the only one who can give legal advice to the corporation. To some extent, you have to divorce yourself from the business team when your lawyer hat is on. Your client is the corporation, not the head of the team developing the business. Your mission is to make sure the legal interests of the corporation are fully vetted and understood.

Steve Krull made a similar point regarding the need for transparency about the reasons he, as General Counsel, was unwilling to support a business initiative:

> I've seen in-house lawyers fall into this trap—they try to derail a bad idea by saying it is too risky from a legal standpoint, when really it isn't—it's just a bad idea for business reasons. That can hurt your reputation. I would just say, "I think this is a bad idea and here is why. It's important to be transparent and to let people know that you're giving honest

legal advice, but you also get to have an opinion about the idea more generally."

Building Relationships and Trust

Establishing credibility does not necessarily go hand-in-hand with popularity. It sometimes can be challenging in any role to be both liked and respected. This can be a particularly difficult challenge for the General Counsel due to the need to retain independence and represent the interests of the corporate client rather than the interests of any one individual. There will be times when those interests collide, which can create tensions in the strongest relationships. Ben Heineman discusses this tension in one of his frequently cited articles:

> General Counsel need credibility and guts—in addition to legal skills and business acumen—when they are playing the role of guardian of the company's integrity and reputation. Ultimately, they are the corporation's lawyer, not the business leader's lawyer. This is a distinction that senior executives may understand intellectually but balk at, because they invariably think their interests and those of the company are the same. Credibility comes, in part, from a GC's character, experience, reputation, self-confidence, and the ability to explain issues forcefully, clearly, and concisely. And it will be strengthened by the basic trust that is created over time by working effectively as a business partner. The hard discussion of limitations and constraints in the present is made easier by business accomplishments in the past.[3]

3. Ben W. Heineman, Jr., *Caught in the Middle*, Corporate Counsel, at 2 (April 2007).

The importance of building trust, as well as advice on how to do it, featured prominently in all of our discussion with the General Counsel we interviewed. We heard that building trust is both a function of credibility and "soft-side" skills. We also heard that it cannot be rushed—it will take some time.

Steve Krull recalled his days at Owens Corning when the company was struggling with the asbestos litigation that forced it into bankruptcy. The board included members of the creditors' committee, whose interests were not necessarily aligned with the long-term prospects of the company, and meetings were frequently confrontational. Steve talked about the importance of developing relationships in navigating his way through those challenges:

> It was all about relationships with board members. I spent a lot of my time calling and visiting individual board members, asking them "What are your concerns, what's on your mind?" I spent time making sure we had opportunities at board meetings for social interaction. I worked on developing cordial relationships with all of the board members. I spent a lot of time listening and socializing, which is not something a lawyer is typically trained to do. These conversations where your motivations are not suspect can allow you to accomplish so much. But you have to be transparent—people have to know they can talk to you candidly. The people I admire most put relationships first.

Brad Thies also focused on the importance of nurturing personal relationships in developing trust with other members of senior management:

> To develop trust, you have to be credible as a business person, reasonable, and you need to be friendly and open. If

people like you as a person, they are more likely to bring their problems to you. If your office is not a place people enjoy coming to visit, you probably are not going to be very effective.

Demonstrating Leadership

The General Counsel role presents many opportunities to demonstrate leadership within and outside the company, and our interviews produced numerous examples of observations about leadership that are interspersed throughout this book. We think Hilary Krane's general comments about leadership offer a framework that seems germane to almost any context in which leadership is discussed: 'As a leader, you don't always ask for permission, you just get it done. People who are successful see something that needs to be done and they do it. If you are always waiting for people to tell you to do something, you won't get very far.'

For NW Natural's MardiLyn Saathoff, demonstrating leadership "is when you know the right thing to do and others may not be entirely on board, but you find successful ways to bring them along." She went on to share examples from her career, which included implementation of robust ethics and compliance programs for her current and former corporate employers. She acknowledged that these programs are not the "sexy stuff" that gets everyone energized and that implementing them often involves mediating competing interests among the Board of Directors, management, and employees about the program's vision, design, and scope. In addition, there are often significant negative biases to be overcome. These are reflected in common reactions like "of course we are an ethical company—why do we need all these bells and whistles?" and in employee concerns about creating a "Big Brother" environment.

Saathoff has managed to lead these implementations successfully in two organizations, earning accolades at the board, management, and employee levels, as well as a reputation as a thought leader in the ethics and compliance field. When asked how she accomplished this, she is quick to point out the importance of "bringing people along." She stresses that it will not work to simply drive these programs as mandates from the board or senior management and that there is a two-way education process that must occur. She must educate her constituencies about the reasons for and benefits of such a program and help them understand the interests of the other stakeholders. The stakeholders, in turn, educate her about the issues that must be addressed to make the program successful. We think her approach represents the essence of leadership.

The Unique Point of View

There are often many views and voices vying for attention at the corporate leadership table, but our successful General Counsel agree that one of the important ways they add value is by having a unique point of view. Amy Schulman described it this way:

> One of the great things about the position is that the General Counsel has an Archimedean point of view. We often are standing above the fray and are able to listen and facilitate synthesizing the competing voices in order to make an enterprise decision. Perhaps that's a way in which we are "generalists." It is impossible to be a great General Counsel if you don't have the ability to draw in different perspectives, be attuned to them, and be flexible enough to adjudicate which viewpoints would be ascendant on a particular issue.

As Schulman's comments reflect, one of the important ways a General Counsel can make a unique contribution to the success of an organization is by mediating different points of view. Significant decisions or initiatives in an organization often involve trade-offs and challenging interactions among the constituencies required to achieve success. For most business decisions, the General Counsel may be able to assume a more neutral role. That ability, when coupled with the critical thinking, negotiation, and persuasion skills that a good General Counsel will possess, makes him or her uniquely well-suited to serve as the "voice of reason."

A related way in which successful General Counsel appear to distinguish themselves is by demonstrating a unique ability to solve problems. Being able to identify and solve problems is critical to the success of an organization. As Jeff Kindler commented: "Companies are about solving problems that are impediments to succeeding in the marketplace. A good General Counsel has to conceive of the role not just in terms of technical proficiency but how to solve problems to help move the business forward."

Fortunately, the desire to solve problems is one of the key characteristics that drives people toward a legal career. As Brad Thies commented:

> If a General Counsel is good, they become a voice of reason and a problem solver, and the law department soon comes to be seen as the "universal problem solver." If you can accomplish that, you will be sought out for advice regarding problems outside of the legal area, and your career satisfaction will be greater.

At the End of the Day

A recent study by Russell Reynolds Associates, a leading global executive search firm, analyzed data from 3,000 assessments administered to executives, including CEOs, CFOs, and GCs, isolating the results of legal officers and comparing them to the results of other executive positions. The findings were published in a report titled "Becoming the Calm Risk Taker: Attributes for Success in Today's New Legal Environment."[4] Among the key findings included in the report was that legal executives differ little from their nonlegal counterparts. The report elaborates on this finding as follows:

> This finding challenges many of the common misperceptions surrounding corporate lawyers—i.e., that they are limited to their technical expertise, fail to fully understand the business, are not proactive, etc. On the contrary, our findings show that the average legal executive is on par with his or her peers on most attributes such as being decisive, setting strategy, executing for results, leading teams, building relationships, and using influence, learning, and thinking and motivating. Organizations looking to hire legal talent should keep these factors in mind lest they set the quality bar too low.

Commenting on the findings in an article that appeared in Corporate Counsel, Cynthia Dow, a member of RRA's legal, government, and regulatory affairs practice, had this to say:

> There is a modernization of in-house legal executives. In recent years, the role of law departments has broadened, requiring GCs to work with the business to evaluate risk and develop corporate strategy. The most strategic conversations

4. Russell Reynolds Associates, *"Becoming the Calm Risk Taker: Attributes for Success in Today's New Legal Environment" Study*, russellreynolds.com, http://www.russellreynolds.com/content/calm-risk-taker-success-in-new-legal-environment.

> are happening within the company and chief legal officers bring a unique perspective to those discussions. They offer a cross-functional and cross-business-unit perspective of the organization, as well as a keen eye toward the external—and increasingly shifting—regulatory environment.[6]

The results of this study and Ms. Dow's comments are consistent with the results of our interviews. Many of the General Counsel we spoke to were quick to point out that the keys to their success were the same as those for any other executive in the organization and downplayed any notion that they were somehow special or unique. As Amy Schulman told us, "I don't really see what I do as unique. To be a good General Counsel is, like all good leaders of enterprise, to bring a perspective to the table while being conscious to forgo the parochial." Perhaps we should add humility to the list?

In the next chapter, we look at another facet of becoming a "Generalist Counsel"—the ability to wear many hats.

6. Shannon Green, *The 8 Characteristics of Successful GCs and CLOs*, law.com, (June, 6, 2012), http://www.law.com/corporatecounsel/PubArticleCC.jsp?id=1202557454809.

7

The Many Hats of the Generalist Counsel

"It used to be that at budget time you would come in and say, 'I need another lawyer.' Then it became—'Here is your budget, hire all the lawyers you want . . . within this budget.' Today it is—'You get money based on the outcomes you plan to generate and your ability to show that the outcomes are worth the investment.'"

MARDILYN SAATHOFF, *Vice President, Legal, Risk and Compliance and Corporate Secretary NW Natural*

Requiring General Counsel to demonstrate Return on Investment is indicative of how the in-house legal function has been forced to manage itself as a business. No longer can the General Counsel say that the only outcome that matters is winning cases. No longer can a General Counsel act as the managing partner of an in-house law firm. No longer is the carrying of the imprimatur of being a lawyer sufficient for survival in a company. And for many, no longer is it acceptable for the General Counsel and her team to act as a support organization to the company—the expectation is now that the in-house legal team is fully integrated into the daily operations of the company—not as an afterthought but as a critical element of business strategy discussions.

These changes are, on balance, viewed by General Counsel as positive. It is undoubtedly preferable to be fully integrated into the business versus being viewed as a cost center that is a necessary evil. However, as Stanley Martin Lieber (Uncle Ben in Spiderman) famously said: "with great power comes great responsibility." The power of involvement and being able to influence strategy carries with it the responsibility of being informed. It carries with it the responsibility of working in a matrix environment with knowledge of disciplines that rely on the law, influence the practice of law in a company, and are impacted by policies and processes the corporate legal department institutes. Today, the General Counsel is somewhat like the Dr. Seuss character Bartholomew Cubbins[1] and is expected to wear 500 hats.

The Chief Operating Officer Hat

The Chief Operating Officer (COO) of a company has to have knowledge of core business management principles and the interdependencies among these principles—an understanding of business processes, people management principles, and knowledge of the core products and services the company offers. Applying this definition in the context of wrangling the complex business issues being handled by (and handed to) the corporate legal department, it is evident that the Generalist Counsel needs to execute his or her role as the COO of the Legal Department.

In a law firm, a senior partner can be a subject matter expert and have relationships with clients where this subject matter expertise is leveraged. This can allow the partner to operate, in relative isolation, in his or her subject area—sometimes for a career spanning decades. Others take care of the administrative and operational aspects of their practice. The partner can just be the subject matter expert—full stop. In a corporation, this same partner, who is now a General Counsel, needs to understand those administrative and operational aspects of legal services delivery.

1. Dr. Seuss, The 500 Hats of Bartholemew Cubbins (1938).

These include, among other things, how legal services are organized, how these services are accessed by the internal clients, how to maximize the efficiency of service delivery, how to manage the cost of service delivery, how to put the right incentive systems in place for the professionals delivering the services, and how to acquire, configure, and deploy the enabling technology that allows the services to be delivered. In other words, the General Counsel needs to operate much like a Chief Operating Officer.

The concept of client satisfaction is not new to any lawyer—after all, a lawyer's traditional function is to serve those who engage them for their expertise and services. However, most law schools still teach students that in a transactional interaction with a client or in managing a litigation matter, the emphasis should be on the delivery of legal advice, grounded in statutes, regulations, and case precedent, as well as reason. There is little discussion of service level agreements that address balancing cost, risk, and cycle time. There is also little discussion about blending legal service delivery resources to optimize the mix of lawyers and nonlawyers involved in a matter. In fact, some law schools (like the alma mater of one of the authors) go out of their way to de-emphasize the commercial aspects of the practice of law, stating instead things like:

> What sets Chicago apart from other law schools is our unabashed enthusiasm for the life of the mind—the conviction that ideas matter, that they are worth discussing, and that legal education should devote itself to learning for learning's sake, not just for earning's sake.[2]

A noble goal, certainly, but one that still leaves the law graduate with a need to acquire other aspects of his or her education that

2. http://www.law.uchicago.edu/school/mission.

will be necessary in the practice of law. There is little discussion about how the delivery of legal services can be made more efficient through the use of technology or technology-enabled processes. In the defense of law school curricula, it is worthy of note that on this last point—technology—a number of law schools are now including legal topics that are impacted by technology as well as some of the practical aspects of using software tools and applications to successfully deliver legal services.[3] However, this is the exception rather than the rule. Understanding that the Generalist Counsel of today needs to think much like a Chief Operating Officer should inspire law schools to step out of their comfort zones and augment curricula to "fit" the more practical aspects of the practice of law.

GC as Chief Strategy Officer

Business strategy discussions have historically emanated from commercial organizations such as sales and marketing. Over the past two decades, technology organizations have also been key drivers of corporate strategy as technology advancements have allowed companies to differentiate and compete along a different dimension. The CFO has also been a key participant in strategy discussions as inorganic opportunities for growth through mergers and acquisitions have become much more pervasive as key elements of a company's growth strategy. Other factors, as

3. See Georgetown Law Curriculum Guide, http://apps.law.georgetown.edu/curriculum/tab_courses.cfm?Status=Course&Detail=2090 (describing a practicum course at Georgetown Law School that "exposes students to the varied uses of computer technologies in the practice of law... [and] familiarizes students with various innovative software platforms that are being adopted in law practice to enhance access to justice, capture legal expertise, interface with clients, manage litigation and transactional processes, and increase the efficiency and quality of legal services.")

discussed below, have resulted in the General Counsel becoming much more involved in corporate strategy over the past decade.

As strategies for growth are put forth, there are often discussions about risks, such as those associated with proposals for business combinations or those relating to expansion into certain markets. Scrutiny of behaviors and practices to ensure that antitrust or other laws are not violated has taken on increasing importance. However, the General Counsel is not just involved to make sure that laws are not violated. General Counsel are privy to ideas and innovations early in their lifecycle through the work done by the legal department's intellectual property teams. Furthermore, any business alliances require contracts and agreements, which are typically negotiated by corporate lawyers working under the General Counsel. As such, General Counsel have visibility to key levers of business growth—organic innovations and business collaborations.

We have seen General Counsel use this knowledge to proactively drive business strategy discussions, in many cases even carrying an official designation as a business or corporate development executive. A case in point is James Dalton, who served for many years as Senior Vice President, Corporate Development, for Tektronix, as well as its General Counsel. Another example is Terry Larkin, Executive Vice President of Business Development and General Counsel of Lear Corporation, a $14 billion corporation that is a leader in the automotive seating and electrical power management industry.

We believe this trend will continue.

The Chief Information Officer Hat

Over the past three decades, the Chief Information Officer (CIO) in the corporation has evolved from being the steward of the company's IT infrastructure to the steward of company data to the steward of company information and company knowledge. "CIOs will need to master four emerging personas in order to compete in the new environment—Chief Infrastructure Officer, Chief Integration Officer, Chief Intelligence Officer and Chief Innovation Officer."[4] This evolution is very similar to the evolution of the role of the General Counsel and is also the driver behind the need to incorporate knowledge of technology as a key dimension of their charter.

Technology has always been present in the corporate legal department. Historically, software applications and tools have been used in these departments for productivity. Litigation teams in particular have been using these technology tools to execute core components of matter-specific work. Litigation support workflow tools, document management, case management, docketing, and other tools have been omnipresent in the office of the General Counsel for decades. General Counsel did not need to understand all the specifics of how these tools worked, but just enough to be able to allocate funding for their acquisition and operation. However, over the past decade, another technology-driven area, resulting from modern tactics in litigation, has dramatically changed the need for a General Counsel to understand technology.

eDiscovery and the General Counsel

eDiscovery, or electronic discovery, refers to the process of identifying, preserving, collecting, reviewing, and producing electronically stored information (ESI) in response to litigation

4. Kristin Burnham, *4 Personas of the Next-Generation CIO*, cio.com (March 2, 2011), http://www.cio.com/article/671573/4_Personas_of_the_Next_Generation_CIO?page=1&taxonomyId=3233.

or compliance-driven discovery requests. For highly litigious companies, or highly regulated companies subject to repeated requests for information, eDiscovery is a fact of daily life. General Counsel have become acutely aware of the cost and risk of eDiscovery, especially when almost seventy percent of total litigation expenditures can be driven by something as seemingly tactical as fulfilling an obligation to produce documents responsive to a discovery request. The enormous volume of ESI being created and stored in companies today has created an often untenable situation for lawyers trying to balance cost, risk, and outcomes.

Perhaps no other discipline has stretched General Counsel more in terms of the need to augment their knowledge of technology. Initially, the need revolved around General Counsel to understand technology that allows the large volume of ESI to be reduced to a level that is affordable for humans to review. Data Reduction, Defensible Collection, Concept Clustering, terabytes, statistical QC, near duplicates, and predictive coding are all terms that most lawyers never heard in law school. However, a more than cursory understanding of these terms has become critical for a General Counsel to properly execute his or her role.

Here are just some of the questions surrounding eDiscovery that are being asked by General Counsel today:

- How can electronic information be collected in a more targeted manner, using technology combined with good old-fashioned lawyerly training?
- How can technology be used to reduce this large corpus of data, once collected and before it is turned over for attorney review?
- How can technology be applied to make the review of these electronic documents more efficient?
- When is the right time to use law firm attorneys to (mechanically) fulfill discovery obligations, and when can

I use a nonlaw firm service provider to do things better, faster, cheaper?

- Are India-based or other offshore services a way to further reduce cost and accelerate cycle time for response?

Years ago, some version of these questions was asked and answered by litigation support teams of law firms. Now, the sheer economic consequences of not understanding how to answer these questions and make the related decisions has compelled General Counsel to delve into a domain formerly reserved for nonlawyer legal support professionals.

eDiscovery as Bridge Builder

On a positive note, eDiscovery has stimulated significant interaction between the Generalist Counsel and the legal department's litigation support or IT/Legal staff, many of whom are nonlawyers. In law firms, despite the importance of their knowledge to the outcome of the litigation process, these professionals sometimes are treated like second-class citizens—perhaps not overtly, but it is our experience that the undertones of this positioning are alive and well. However, in the corporate setting, these techno-legal individuals have been instrumental in providing the General Counsel with knowledge about eDiscovery, a domain that is the quintessential law-technology intersection issue. Litigation support staff understands not only technology but also its application in the legal context. And this knowledge has elevated the stature of these individuals in the General Counsel's eyes.

Leveraging this knowledge has allowed General Counsel to think and speak cogently in areas that impact the legal process but are historically the domain of nonlawyer technical personnel. Topics such as the mechanics of privilege logging and redactions, the technology used to collect data and documents from corporate computers in a legally defensible manner, the difference between structured and unstructured data—have all become a part of the General Counsel's parlance. This has actually been a good thing for General Counsel because knowledge of this techno-legal domain has turned out to be a great foundation for tackling even more hairy techno-legal challenges; in the process creating the positive side effect of causing a senior lawyer to appreciate the talents and contributions of a community of nonlawyers who are still fighting for their rightful place within law firms.

Information Governance

eDiscovery has focused attention on the cost, risks, technology, and processes associated with fulfilling one's obligations when compelled to produce information as part of a litigation- or compliance-related discovery process. Very quickly, companies realized that the root cause of the cost and risk associated with eDiscovery response lay in the *practices, policies and behaviors* of company employees in the *creation, storage and management* of this electronically stored information—in other words, Information Governance. As such, the General Counsel was brought into conversations (often, these days, the General Counsel creates these conversations) that focused on domains typically reserved for the CIO of the company.

Take for example, the intellectual property lifecycle in a company. Ideas may originate from every nook and cranny in a company. These ideas are brought to a forum where they can be vetted, and some crack team of engineers, or researchers, or product managers put some form and function around the idea(s). A marketer... or ten... determine the commercial viability of this (product or service) idea. Some ideas make it through the "return on investment churn-mill" and are then brought to market. The idea starts generating revenue and is a blockbuster drug, valve, motor, consulting methodology, claims processing IT-enabled service, child care center... AND it results in significant profit to the company. Then... somebody sues the company....

The product or service doesn't do (allegedly) what it is purported to do. The company has deep pockets because the product or service is commercially successful. Plaintiffs' attorneys are able to get a large group of individuals all "lathered up" about the possibility of collecting thousands of dollars for the "alleged wrongs perpetrated upon the unsuspecting consumer." Class action lawsuits are filed. Document preservation obligations kick in. All of a sudden, the General Counsel and his in-house legal team realize that there is a vast universe of data and documents (information) that is potentially in scope as part of a legal discovery request.

Root Cause

None of this information would have existed if not created. It would not exist if it were not stored. It would not exist if it were deleted when it reached its normal retention "half-life." The General Counsel is at the tip of the arrow to resolve these challenges and... pay the bill to do so. This is the environment of (today's) Generalist Counsel and prompts the GC to conjure up all sorts of "doomsday" scenarios that shape their point of view on how they need to insure the optimal balance between a command and control mentality—when it comes to the creation, management and storage of data—and one that enables the proper management of risk while ensuring that the culture of the company is accommodated... or else.

The General Counsel has approached these challenges by becoming knowledgeable about things such as the company's records retention practices. These topics are born from functions such as facilities management, where warehouse management personnel originally created a "schedule" outlining which types of boxes of paper records should be destroyed first to make room for more boxes coming in from the cubes and offices of corporate staff. These days, the records retention schedule is a valuable tool in the GC's arsenal—one that allows him to regulate the policies and practices surrounding the storage and destruction of documents in the corporation, which eventually could result in lower legal expenditure and even affect the outcomes of litigation matters.

Cracking the Code

Fortunately, there are myriad knowledge sources for today's Generalist Counsel to get education and support on these seemingly enigmatic issues. There are technology and consulting companies lining up to educate the GC on topics such as Information Governance, Records and Information Management, Information Risk Management—basically anything that results in an acronym. This doesn't mean, "buyer, beware." Rather, a Generalist Counsel should avail himself of these resources but realize that each resource has an angle as a commercial organization that wants to sell technology and services to the corporation, using the Generalist Counsel's point of view on enterprise risk as their selling value proposition. The General Counsel needs to learn how to deal with technology and service vendors and assess which products and services would be most appropriate to assist in the Information Governance challenge. He needs to understand that technology is not an elixir but is something that enables the functioning of a business process. Technology acquisition efforts should start with a detailed understanding of business requirements that are accompanied by process maps outlining the inputs and outputs of the process. There should be responsibility matrices put in place to outline "who does what to whom." Nothing in these activity sets remotely resembles what a senior partner may have done, much less had exposure to, in a law firm. So, what is a General Counsel to do? Partner with the Chief Information Officer, of course.

Intersection of Technology and Law—Generalist Counsel as Bridge

The partnership between the GC and the CIO has never been more important. We have talked a lot about the need for the Generalist Counsel to understand and incorporate technology in his management of the legal function. The converse is also true. The CIO has an important need to understand the implications of legal and compliance matters on technology strategy. The Generalist Counsel's ability to act as a bridge between technology and the law is essential to the CIO's ability to succeed in this domain.

Take, for example, the CIO's need to implement an enterprise content management system to support the organization's need for collaboration and knowledge sharing (also known as knowledge management). Most companies have a very federated (and often fragmented and disparate) web of content management systems. In other words, most companies do not have one unified place for user-created documents and information to be stored. Different lines of business and geographies, over time, may have acquired their own systems, instituted their own practices, and put in place their own policies for where content should be stored.

As such, many CIO's are looking at ways to centralize content storage—not just for cost savings reasons (actual hardware and software costs of storing electronic information is getting less expensive day by day) but more to reduce the risk associated with a disparate content management universe that makes it cumbersome to manage stored information in a strategic manner. It is difficult to locate information needed. When located, it may be complex to determine which version of the content is the "gold master" version. Once determined, it may be technically challenging to retrieve the content from the source and put it in a format that is consumable. Most importantly, it is likely very difficult to apply the company's records retention schedule to content that is stored in many different places across the organization.

Considerations in Content Management Strategy Execution

In the process of formulating and executing this content management strategy, the CIO needs to be keenly aware of the risks and challenges of information management. What content is considered an official company record? What content, if not disposed of in a timely manner, with defensible processes, creates undue risk for the company? What functionality in a content management application creates challenges for the company? Case in point: there have been a number of rulings in litigation matters involving electronic discovery holding that if video conferencing software does not have in-built functionality to record a conference, a company is not required to programmatically augment the software to enable same. Courts have said, in essence, that a company does not need to create a record if a record wouldn't ordinarily exist as part of normal business operations. How do these types of rulings impact not just the type of content management system the CIO purchases but also the configuration and implementation strategy for the system? Does the CIO feel comfortable putting up herself or one of her leaders as the go-to deponent when questions about these practices arise? Where does the CIO go for guidance? The Generalist Counsel is the most likely source for the CIO to ask and answer these "bridge" questions.

Policy "Wonk" Hat

Law firm lawyers are often called upon by General Counsel to weigh in on the contents of corporate policies and procedures that have significant risk management implications for the company. However, when occupying the General Counsel seat, policies and procedures take on a different dimension.

It is not just the legal risks, defensibility, and transparency elements of policies that need to be considered but also the readability, practicality, cost of implementation, and enforceability of the policy, among other considerations. After all, a Generalist Counsel is an executive of the corporation and ultimately needs to ensure that any policies emanating from the legal department (and often elsewhere) are consistent with the culture of the organization and can actually withstand the test of usability. These are some of the questions a General Counsel needs to answer:

- Should the policy be made available to all employees or only to select affected employees?
- How should the policy be disseminated/communicated? Should it be available on the corporate intranet? Should it be sent to all employees via email?
- Should there be a formal policy rollout that includes training? Should the training be mandatory?
- How will compliance with the policy be assured? Is an enforcement and verification mechanism necessary?
- How will the effectiveness of the policy be judged and who will be the adjudicator?

None of these considerations is likely to be a material element of a policy review conducted by an outside lawyer. They require consideration by someone who understands and appreciates the nuances of these considerations in the context of the corporate culture.

Leader and Culture Czar Hat

Let's switch to a "softer" topic: motivating, focusing, and inspiring people. In a law firm, informal partner-associate mentoring relationships are generally relied on for motivating, inspiring, and focusing more junior lawyers in the firm. This may be justified to some extent by the fact that the duties of an associate are generally self-evident: do what the senior partner tells you to do in service of the client and make sure you record your hours, although there is ample evidence that many law firm associates are not very satisfied with the quality or effectiveness of this approach.[5] In contrast, a Generalist Counsel needs to set the tone and mission for the entire legal department to ensure that members of the team are aligned, moving synchronously and consistently with the larger objectives of the organization. The mission must be conveyed to team members in a way that is understandable and galvanizes them around common goals. And, of course, the legal department mission needs to directly connect to the mission, values and core business objectives of the company. Compensation systems need to be aligned with actions taken in support of the mission.

James Lipscomb shared with us some of his strategies for ensuring appropriate alignment of MetLife's legal department with the mission of the business. One important element of his

5. See Wilkins, Ch. 1, *supra* note 7, at 2108 ("One of the most important promises that firms make to those whom they recruit is that they will provide these young lawyers with excellent training in the skills and dispositions that they need to become accomplished and skilled practitioners. In recent years, however, this promise has grown increasingly illusory.")

strategy was to give his team a role in creating the vision and mission for the legal department. As he said, "I did not give my lawyers a vision—they worked with me to create a vision, which was 'proactive professional partnerships for committed people.'" Underlying that vision was the principle that "every voice in the room counts" because people are much more likely to respond to a vision that they have had a hand in creating. He also stressed the importance of demonstrating his commitment to the people working for him to inspire their commitment to the business. "They have to see that you will advocate for them. You have to be committed to them to make sure they are committed to the company."

This approach represents the type of executive leadership demanded of a Generalist Counsel and reflects what is perhaps the most important element of leadership: the leader must "walk the talk."

In addition to ensuring alignment with values and mission, a Generalist Counsel must also understand the brand personality of the company and imbue this brand and the associated corporate culture into the legal department. Lawyers are not naturally sensitized to dimensions of corporate culture—this is a learned trait that often requires hard work to absorb. NIKE's Hilary Krane commented on the importance of culture and brand personality in the context of the similarities and differences between NIKE and her former employer, Levi Strauss & Co.:

> Levi's and NIKE at their cores are very similar, but here are some significant differences, such the sheer scale of NIKE and the IP intensity. NIKE is a brand protection organization with a much faster business cycle. And then, of course, there is culture. Levi is a lifestyle company. NIKE is a sports company. From a legal standpoint, the challenges are similar but the cultural uniqueness needs to be understood.

Krane went on to say that she viewed as critical to the success of the legal department the ability of the lawyers to communicate with the business in a way that conveyed their understanding of NIKE culture and brand identity. These are issues of paramount importance to the business and the businesspeople need to know that their lawyers understand and appreciate them.

Brad Thies illustrated his understanding of the importance of adapting legal advice to the cultural context by sharing with us some of the challenges he has had in implementing solid intellectual property protection practices, which are critical in a scientific instruments company like FEI. He told us that it is the culture of the scientists to "want to share everything. In an ideal world, they see everyone collaborating. It goes against the grain of our culture to enhance corporate value through better IP protection, but it has to be done."

Thies decided to use an opportunity presented by a patent infringement suit in which FEI sued a competitor to get his message across more effectively. He found that when he explained the circumstances surrounding the lawsuit to his scientists, their views changed significantly. "They weren't so concerned about someone else using our IP, but they were morally outraged that someone had claimed to have invented something we developed here." Thies told us that the case was settled on a favorable basis, but that the real victory was in his ability to change attitudes: "We won way more internally than we did with the settlement because the case served to strip away some of the naïveté that had existed previously."

The Arbiter and Voice of Reason Hat

General Counsel are often called upon to lead the charge for incident response in the face of a crisis—to be the corporate crisis manager. We have only to open the newspaper on any given day to see one or more examples of a crisis that has the potential to severely damage the reputation of a company and generate other unwelcome consequences. Increasingly, the crisis often revolves around a "personal" scandal that somehow evolves into something that has the potential to cast doubt on the integrity of an entire organization. Such was the case when Michael Holston, General Counsel of Hewlett-Packard Company, was placed in the midst of a crisis caused by HP's former CEO Mark Hurd's inappropriate relationship with a contractor. Hurd resigned from his HP post amid allegations that he had sexually harassed a former actress and reality-television personality who had worked for HP as a marketing consultant. Although a company investigation concluded that Hurd did not violate the company's sexual-harassment policies, the investigation found that Hurd had submitted inaccurate expense reports attempting to conceal his personal relationship with the contractor and that the contractor was at times paid for nonexistent work.

Holston, who publicly pronounced these indiscretions as breaches of "integrity, credibility and honesty,"[6] succeeded in positioning Hurd's transgressions as the failing of one person and not a fundamental values issue for the company. Holston's handling of the situation required a delicate balancing act. Billions of dollars of economic value could have been lost if Hurd's actions had been allowed to undermine the integrity of the organization, but Holston also had a responsibility to be fair to a man who was not just his boss but was married with two children.

Another recent example of a General Counsel effectively leading an organization through a crisis involved the 2012 lockout of referees who officiate National Football League games, causing replacement referees to become the centerpiece of conversations. Jeff Pash, General Counsel for the National Football League, was put in the unenviable position of lead negotiator

6. http://news.cnet.com/8301-31021_3-20012944-260.html.

with the representatives of the locked out referees. In essence, Pash's task was to figure out how to balance a $3 million compensation exposure with the negative publicity being showered upon the multi-billion dollar American football industry. This was a crisis of wide-ranging proportions where opinions were put forth from corner offices, cubicles, commodes, and couches. One wrong move resulting in the alienation of fans could have resulted in billions of dollars of economic losses. The ability of Pash to remain calm in the face of chaos was a critical component of the eventual successful resolution of this crisis.

This ability to maintain calm and exercise careful judgment in a crisis situation often places General Counsel in the role of arbiter. In a situation involving conflict or a significant business decision over which there are widely divergent points of view, General Counsel are well suited for the role of arbiter, where they can use, as Amy Schulman termed it, their Archimedean point of view.

Other Critical Roles

We have focused in this chapter on some of the "business roles" that General Counsel are increasingly expected to master. Of course, there are many other important roles, both formal and informal, that are played by a General Counsel. These include the more traditional lawyer roles such as legal advisor and client advocate, certain quasi-legal roles such as compliance officer and corporate ethics officer, and other management and leadership roles, including the very important roles of corporate officer and liaison to the Board of Directors. These roles and some of the tensions underlying their execution are beyond the scope of this chapter but have been the subject of several excellent works.[7]

7. See *Indispensable Counsel*, Ch. 3, *supra* note 2. See also, Duggin, Ch. 1, *supra* note 1; and DeMott, Introduction, *supra* note 2.

8

Roadmap to the Top

"[In response to your question asking whether General Counsel are uniquely qualified to be Chief Executive Officers], there are as many reasons to choose a General Counsel to be CEO as not. What you look for in a leader is a clear, decisive thinker, a good communicator, a motivator of people and an assessor of risk and opportunity. Some lawyers have those skills in abundance, others don't. In the 1960s there were quite a few GCs who became CEOs. In part it's a matter of orientation of skill sets and opportunity."

AMY SCHULMAN, *Executive Vice President and General Counsel, Pfizer Inc.*

We agree with Schulman that a fully formed Generalist Counsel has as much right to aspire to be CEO as any other senior executive, but simply having been a General Counsel does not qualify anyone to be Chief Executive. And, while we also agree that the ascendancy from General Counsel to the CEO position is not something new, we do believe there are factors at play in business today that may create the perfect environment for General Counsel to move into CEO roles with increasing frequency. In this chapter, we explore that thesis by looking at some examples of General Counsel who succeeded in making the transition to CEO. We also outline some macro themes that we believe will contribute to an increase in these transitions. We do this by focusing on storytelling. As we have discovered, and as validated by our storytellers, there is no "playbook" for making the transition from General Counsel to CEO and every situation is different.

We make observations where we think they are helpful, but in many cases, we let the story speak for itself.

Rearranging the Building Blocks

We have certainly given Jeff Kindler a lot of attention in this book, and for good reason. Kindler represents one of the more high-profile examples of General Counsel to Generalist Counsel to CEO. His tenure as CEO of pharmaceuticals giant Pfizer has been thoroughly documented and dissected by the media. But less well-known were the years he spent as head of a commercial business unit at McDonald's, where, he says, he gained some of the business leadership experience that actually prepared him to run a major public corporation and helped to reshape his decision-making framework.

"First you have to change the mindset that lawyers have. There is the assumption from all that legal training that the law produces answers to questions that will give themselves up if you apply enough work. It is what you are trained to believe and do," Kindler told us.

He went on to say:

> In business, it is quite different, especially either in the early stages of entrepreneurial operations or the later stages of very mature organizations. There simply are no clear answers to profound questions. As a business leader, I'm not looking for a right answer but the best decision based upon the circumstances.
>
> The second thing is operating experience. There is not any substitute for operating and profit and loss experience. The difference is huge between being an advisor and being

the person who has the ultimate responsibility for P&L and general management. Anyone who is aspiring to be a business leader should try to acquire that P&L experience.

Industry Agnostic or Industry Specific?

One question we asked all interviewees was whether they believed there was a glass ceiling within corporations that prevents a General Counsel from ascending all the way to the top. There seemed to be general agreement that, for the most part, any glass ceiling has disappeared. However, some of our sources believe the pathway to the top for the General Counsel is clearer in some industries than in others.

Peter Bragdon of Columbia Sportswear believes consumer goods companies like Columbia will want someone with a strong product marketing background in the hot seat. Brad Thies at FEI thinks his lack of a scientific background would make him an unlikely CEO candidate for a company that operates in such a highly scientific and technical space. Automobile companies tend to select executives with lots of marketing experience. But in highly regulated industries such as pharmaceuticals, utilities, insurance, and transportation, where legal and regulatory issues abound and the legal department is closely connected to developing strategy for the company, the path to the top for the ambitious lawyer seems somewhat easier to see.

"The lawyers have been brought more into that decision-making process over the years," says MetLife's Nicholas Latrenta. "In our company we have had two General Counsel who started in the law department and became CEOs. Our current CEO and the previous one had the lawyer training. In our world the lawyer skill set is a good one to have."

Margaret Kirkpatrick at NW Natural points out that the politically inclined General Counsel represents a strong candidate for CEO in utilities firms where senior executives are constantly interacting with regulators. "Two of our prior CEOs, Mark Dodson and Bob Ridgely, were lawyers. A willingness to learn what they didn't know put them in good position to be CEO. The legal skill set is a great one to have in this business."

But, according to Schnitzer Steel's Rich Josephson, the corporate lawyer with CEO aspirations must balance an ingrained "seek the whole truth and nothing but the truth" orientation with big picture visioning and creative problem solving in order to be CEO material. As Josephson said:

> I've seen it all and I don't think whether you're a lawyer or not is outcome determinative. Obviously lawyers tend to be very analytical. There's something of a challenge there—you need someone who can think out of the box to be a CEO and that isn't something that comes naturally to some of us. There have been some highly successful lawyers who became CEOs—it's a question of whether you develop that range of abilities. It's almost as though if you are a lawyer, you have to *overcome* that linear thinking to become a CEO.

Jeff Kindler

Now, back to Jeff Kindler. As both a former General Counsel and CEO, Kindler brings both the ground level and the 10,000-foot view to the question of what best prepares a lawyer for the corner office. He sought to disabuse us of the notion that General Counsel are more likely to be considered for a CEO slot if they are in a highly regulated industry—in other words he does not believe that a General Counsel in a highly regulated business can make a better case for becoming CEO than in a nonregulated industry.

> It is true some people think a regulated industry is part of it, but I really do think that is wrong. In a regulated industry, you'd better have a good General Counsel independent of the CEO. It is not the CEO's job to provide that regulatory advice. And my second point would be: Is there such a thing as an unregulated industry? Some are more regulated than others, but no industry is unaffected by the actions of policy makers.

Credentialing

Jeff Kindler argues that it is neither the industry in which one labors nor one's training, but rather the determination to add broader value to the business and in the process acquiring broader business skills that will prepare the General Counsel to move beyond the corporate legal department.

> There are a lot of respects in which lawyers are not suited to be business people due to their training. They tend to be trained to be precise. In law school, as associates of law firms, and in legal associations where the principal role is legal research, you have to find the supposed answers to questions that are thought to be answerable by statutes and regulations. As a business leader, you are making judgments about a course of action you should or shouldn't take. Those decisions are about experience and intuition. They don't lend themselves to going into a library and looking up an answer. So as you get more senior as a lawyer or business person, you have to get it into your mind that it is all about making the best decision versus finding the right answer.

Kindler believes the General Counsel who aspires to the role of CEO should ask: Am I gaining experience at weighing risks and taking calculated risks in order to move the enterprise forward? He said:

> When you get to the point as General Counsel where you feel comfortable giving advice like that, recognizing that there is no absolute answer or way to look it up, then you may be ready. It all comes down to your judgment and experience and pattern recognition. That is a skill set that will serve you well going from lawyer to CEO because that is what CEOs do every single day. The decisions that come to CEOs are ones that have no clear definitive answer.

By logging as much business experience as possible, the General Counsel who is most likely to be effective as a CEO can enhance his or her training for the job. Kindler's career path demonstrates this. Kindler spent much of his time during the 1990s continually searching for ways to add value to the business at large, while bringing many innovations to his legal departments at General Electric and later at McDonald's. It was at McDonald's where he got his first taste of life after the law when he was named President of the fast food giant's Partner Brands, which included the Boston Market and Chipotle chains.

It was with this resume now enriched with business leadership credentials that Kindler joined Pfizer as its General Counsel, where he faced even greater career challenges and opportunities. Although he was initially not considered the front-runner to replace the retiring CEO, Hank McKinnell, Kindler was ultimately selected by the board and became Chairman and CEO of Pfizer in 2006. As with any high profile position, his four-year tenure was not without controversy, but, overall, he will be remembered for managing the acquisition of Wyeth, for playing an important role as a spokesperson for broader industry issues, including health care reform, and for driving operational efficiency to prepare the company for an environment where the heyday of cash making branded pharmaceutical companies was fast coming to a close.

Managing the Spotlight

Kindler's selection as Pfizer's CEO was a tribute to the attention he paid to adding value not only as the leader of the legal department but also to the business at large. He sought out opportunities like the Partner Brands position to gain management experience so that he could be a better General Counsel. He made sure that, as General Counsel, he acted as a trusted advisor to the CEO and the board—a status obtained by exercising good judgment, providing good counsel, and ensuring that his lens was broader than the legal department. And he was considered to be an innovator as General Counsel.

When asked if he could offer advice about how to handle the enormous visibility that comes with the transition to CEO, especially at a major publicly held company such as Pfizer, he said there was little to give:

> When you are center stage, going from General Counsel to CEO, it's awfully hard to prepare for it. To be candid, it may not be the best way to do things. Generally speaking, being the CEO of a major company is one of the more difficult roles you can imagine. The scope of responsibility and the number of stakeholders makes the CEO position unlike any other job one can imagine having. There is hardly anything you can do to prepare for it except to be COO for a year or two and be in the shadow of the CEO. Either having been a CEO or having understudied to one is the single best way to prepare for a job that is order of magnitude harder than any other business position.

Kindler also added: "The visibility is just one element of it. Even if you are a direct report to the CEO, and you have a very big job and a lot of responsibility—that is still just a slice of a gigantic pie that you are suddenly responsible for when you become CEO."

Other Stories

Although we did not interview the next few individuals who also ascended from General Counsel to CEO, we also found their stories to be instructive and share them here.

Angela Braly

For Angela Braly, the former Chairman and CEO of WellPoint, the pathway to the corner office did not take the same twists and turns that Jeff Kindler's did, but ultimately, she sat in the seat for only a short while. Having achieved CEO status, she held on to it for five years, only to be toppled by shareholder unrest over subpar financial returns.

A native of Dallas, Braly received her JD from Southern Methodist University School of Law. She made partner at the St. Louis law firm of Lewis, Rice & Fingersh, L.C. In 1999, she transitioned from law firm to corporation, joining WellPoint as General Counsel for RightCHOICE (now Anthem Blue Cross and Blue Shield in Missouri). It was the ideal environment for someone with a legal background—lots of regulatory terrain to navigate, opportunities to manage a major healthcare player's government relations, and an opportunity to be involved in structuring complex deals.

Braly is generally credited with masterminding the legal strategy behind the formation of The Missouri Foundation for Health, which provides coverage for the underinsured and uninsured in Missouri, and she was later named president and CEO of the foundation. By then, her executive credentials had been well established.

In 2007, Braly was named Chairman and CEO of WellPoint, the second largest health insurer in the United States, with revenue exceeding $60 billion. This was an extremely challenging time in the health insurance industry. The industry was in the spotlight when healthcare reform became a political battlefield as legislators and the White House were driving toward an overhaul of the entire health insurance industry in the United States.

Against this backdrop, Braly championed strategic initiatives designed to create revenue streams from new products and services as well as to limit exposure to existing lines of business that were dragging margins down. These were areas of focus far removed from the practice of law and required her to demonstrate her proficiency with marketing and service line development. She understood that this was not a time for a focus on risk and controls but instead on top line growth. However, despite her bold actions executed with full support of her board of directors, profits continued to disappoint investors. As Jeff Kindler stated, success in managing a P&L (in this case a $60 Billion P&L) is measured by business results using barometers like EBITDA rather than success in quelling regulatory turbulence. In addition, she had the unpleasant task of personally defending premium increases before public agencies and forums, appearances that saddled her with the burden of being the bearer of bad tidings. Bowing to pressure from investors, she resigned from WellPoint in August 2012.

Despite WellPoint's challenges, Braly's ambitious and often innovative efforts to restructure the company underscored the value of a legal background for a corporate executive in a highly regulated industry. However, Braly's legacy goes far beyond her transition from lawyer to CEO, which has kept her in the spotlight in positive ways. She has served as a role model for other women with CEO aspirations. During her tenure as Chairman and CEO of WellPoint, Braly was the only woman to head a Fortune 50 corporation. *Fortune*, *Forbes*, and the *St. Louis Business Journal* have all recognized her as among the most powerful women in business.

Lloyd Blankfein

Visibility does not seem to have taken its toll on another high-profile lawyer-turned-executive who holds the reins of power at one of the world's most powerful financial services firms.

It has been more than three decades since Lloyd Blankfein actively practiced law. But his legal background no doubt proved to be a valuable asset as he navigated a path from corporate tax lawyer to Chairman and CEO of Goldman Sachs Group. Blankfein never sat in the General Counsel seat, but he was trained in the law and was able to use his academic grounding and his law firm training to support tremendous career success in a domain that is vastly different from the practice of law.

Blankfein came up the hard way, growing up in a blue-collar household in the Bronx projects. Both parents worked just to make ends meet, and their example of hard work as a way of life made a lasting impression on their son. Bright and ambitious, he earned his BA and JD from Harvard and was hired to practice tax law by the white-shoe New York firm Donovan, Leisure, Newton & Irvine. But life in the law firm was not for Blankfein, who set his sights on a career in banking. He made the transition from law firm to corporation in 1981, joining Goldman's commodities trading division, J. Aron & Co. as a salesman in London.

By 1994, he was in charge of the trading division and had been clearly marked as an executive with a future at Goldman. When the firm launched its Fixed Income, Currency and

Commodities Division (FICC) in 1997, Blankfein was tapped to manage it. Seven years later, he moved up to President and Chief Operating Officer of Goldman Sachs and in 2006 was named its Chairman and CEO.

Despite challenges to his leadership and the investigations and lawsuits that resulted from the financial markets meltdown, Blankfein survived to attain elder statesman status once the dust began to settle. The role his legal training may have played in his ability to weather the legal storms resulting from the financial crisis is unclear, but the fact that Blankfein retained his grip on power during that tumultuous period suggests at a minimum that the savvy lawyer/CEO chose his own legal team wisely.

Frank Blake

Diversity seems to be the spice of Frank Blake's life. From his early days as a freshly minted Harvard graduate working for the Massachusetts legislature to his current position as Chairman and CEO of Home Depot, Blake has demonstrated a strong penchant for exploring new challenges. He has been back and forth between government and private sector jobs, and within those two sectors, he has changed roles constantly. His long tenure in the retail industry, which began in 2002, is the first sign that perhaps Frank Blake has finally found a home at Home Depot.

Though several of our lawyer-CEOs have taken complicated routes to the top, Blake's is worth noting in some detail. His quiet, aw-shucks persona, which has served him well during controversial times at Home Depot, belies a compelling ambition to see and do it all during his corporate life. From his first job to his latest, here is his curriculum vitae:

- Legislative assistant to the joint committee on social welfare, Massachusetts legislature

- Law clerk, Judge Wilfred Feinbert
- Law clerk to Justice John Paul Stevens, U.S. Supreme Court
- Deputy Counsel, Vice President George H. W. Bush
- General Counsel, U.S. Environmental Protection Agency
- General Counsel, GE Power Systems
- Vice President of Business Development, GE Power Systems
- Senior Vice President, General Electric Co.
- Deputy Secretary, US Department of Energy
- Executive Vice President of Business Development and Corporate Operations, Home Depot, Inc.
- Vice Chairman of the Board of Directors, Home Depot, Inc.
- Chairman and CEO, Home Depot, Inc.

Blake crossed paths with Kindler while at GE, but other than that, his career trajectory could be safely called unique when compared to that of the General Counsel we interviewed and profiled in this book. Leaving a position of corporate clout at GE to return to the public sector, where he had already served several times, might seem incongruous to an executive seeking power and a healthy compensation package, but Blake has used his combination of legal expertise and corporate experience to satisfy his proclivity for testing his abilities in new forums. He constantly sought out roles to hone his business chops and gain experiences that would allow him to be "business accountable."

When Blake was tapped to run Home Depot in 2002, the selection confounded retail industry experts, given his lack of retail experience. He replaced Bob Nardelli, known for his aggressive and, many say, abrasive style. Blake's reputation was as an executive who listened and managed collaboratively, a 180-degree shift from Nardelli's way of doing things. By all accounts,

Blake has handled controversy and corporate restructuring with aplomb, inspiring one admirer to dub him "calmer-in-chief." Blake reportedly sends handwritten thank-you notes to Home Depot "associates," has a monthly live call-in TV show open to all associates, makes his email address available to all who ask and actually responds to the emails he receives. In addition, he has generally overseen tough calls with a tolerant, humble style that has won him the admiration of many Home Depot employees and customers. When someone suggests that lawyers are a bit lacking in the empathy department, you may wish to respond with a suggestion that they read up on calmer-in-chief, Frank Blake.

Smartest guy in the room? Blake likely is, but he would just as likely be reluctant to claim this moniker.

Brian Moynihan

Brian Moynihan, CEO of Bank of America, is another legally trained CEO of a major financial institution who was thrust into a power position only to face true fiscal crises. There, Moynihan has demonstrated a flair for bold actions in times of trouble. Whether or not his strategic machinations on behalf of Bank of America will keep the financial Titanic from floundering remains to be seen.

Moynihan received his JD from Notre Dame Law School, but seems to have viewed his legal training principally in terms of how it could assist him in his quest to be a well-rounded corporate executive. From what we have read and observed, he has always been more a banker than a lawyer, although he's occasionally been asked to dust off the law books when lawyering was in short supply.

Moynihan joined Fleet Bank soon after leaving behind the bucolic Notre Dame campus, initially taking the legal route into the corporate world. As his career unfolded in the 1990s, he was moved out of law and into corporate strategy, where he found his true calling. He was a key player in Fleet's expansion and, when Fleet was acquired by Bank of America in 2004, he was asked to stay on by the new owner. As president of Bank of America's global wealth/investment management operations, he helped resolve legal issues brought on by overly aggressive fund managers. His reward: head honcho of Bank of America's global corporate and investment bank. That was in 2007, and he found himself reporting to Bank of America's then CEO Ken Lewis, whose reputation is legendary. Lewis asked Moynihan to take on the General Counsel responsibilities to help deal with the fall-out of the 2008 financial crisis—General Counsel in the familiar role of crisis manager (see Chapter Seven). But Lewis would soon run afoul of investors as Bank of America's acquisition of Merrill Lynch unraveled, and Moynihan would quickly box up the legal books once more.

Following the exit of Lewis in 2009, Moynihan assumed the CEO role as one of the few banking executives around willing to take on the cleanup of the massive financial institution. Again, crisis manager, albeit of a scope and scale that few General Counsel or CEOs can imagine facing. Moynihan has been at it ever since, wheeling and dealing, perhaps not quite with Lewis's oft-cited imperious manner, but not without a certain in-your-face style of his own. It is almost as if has unleashed the inner litigator that was never allowed to have a place in Moynihan's career, but was always lurking. Moynihan may have been able to exercise this penchant in Bank of America's recent $11.6 billion settlement with Fannie Mae relating to its mortgage practices.

At this writing, Moynihan still has a grip on the reins of power at Bank of America. But even if he and his employer were to part ways, there would likely be no shortage of Fortune 50 corporations clamoring for the services of this Generalist Counsel turned CEO.

The Road Ahead

Looking ahead, many of those we interviewed believe the time is not far off when legal training will be viewed as a critical skill set for a CEO candidate. Today, we were told, the future leaders of corporations are being groomed in the corporate law department.

P.D. Villarreal thinks the emergence of a larger crop of General Counsel CEO candidates is "inevitable." "As the role of the law department expands and the General Counsel is routinely at the table with other senior management, they will increasingly be seen as legitimate candidates," he said. "Some will be able to show how adept they are at the *business part of the business*. And they will make that move."

Though Villarreal insists he has no CEO aspirations, he says this: "It seems to hit a General Counsel at some point in their career that there's one more step they'd like to take. Companies have increasingly come to understand that so much of what they do has a legal aspect to it. As a result, the influence of the General Counsel has grown."

"We have talked for a long time about how lawyers need to learn more about business," he adds. "But we may have reached the phase where that's no longer the case. Now, perhaps the business people need to learn about the law rather than the lawyers needing to learn about the business."

We agree with Villarreal that the trend of General Counsel ascending to the CEO seat is likely to intensify as investors and the public and regulatory agencies increase their scrutiny of corporations and the behavior of corporate executives. The dual impacts of increased regulation and globalization will continue to increase the complexity of doing business and highlight the need for risk/value-based judgment in business decision making. Crisis management will continue to be a highly valued skill set in our 24–7 news cycle where new corporate wrongdoings seem to be unearthed every day, with the potential to have devastating impact on company reputations and earnings. The public distaste for and enhanced scrutiny of the financial services industry will continue to cry out for reassuring, ethical leadership. The convergence of these factors will place analytic thinking, sound judgment, an ethos of fundamental fairness and justice, and a strong work ethic in high demand. Of course, these qualities are by no means the exclusive domain of lawyers, but they represent the aspirational values of the strong General Counsel.

9

A Note of Caution

"There are so many great things about this job, but the risks involved are tremendous. I'm not sure people understand how much these jobs have changed. Much more is expected and it's not just that there is more regulation."

PETER BRAGDON, *Senior Vice President, Legal and Corporate Affairs, General Counsel, Secretary, Columbia Sportswear*

With every boon comes a bane. In the case of a Generalist Counsel, it is accepting not just the opportunities but also the risks associated with holding the position. These risks make it necessary to have a capable person in the seat. On the opportunity side, some of the more pervasive themes to emerge from our interviews are the following:

- General Counsel must deeply immerse themselves in the business in order to do their jobs effectively—making them better executives overall.
- General Counsel are expected to weigh in with strategic business advice as well as legal advice, which gives them the opportunity to be "in the room" when the important discussions are occurring.
- General Counsel must build trust and confidence with other members of the management team in order to do their jobs effectively.
- General Counsel are there to anticipate and help remove obstacles that may impede the business from moving forward, which gives them the opportunity to contribute directly to company performance.

These themes are, for the most part, reflective of the more positive aspects of the General Counsel role. But what about those situations—hopefully rare—in which moving the business forward may be in conflict with the equally important role of protecting the corporation's integrity and reputation? The General Counsel we interviewed did not highlight this as a significant area of challenge for them personally. Perhaps this is not surprising given that openly discussing such challenges could involve public disclosure of confidential or sensitive information. However, many of them addressed this issue in a more indirect way.

It Comes with the Territory

Many of the General Counsel we interviewed spoke about the importance of making sure they are part of a senior management team that values establishing and maintaining an ethical culture. They also stressed the importance of having the support of the CEO and the Board to speak frankly and, if necessary, advise against an ill-advised course of action. There was also clear consensus that the General Counsel role—particularly in a public company—presents complex challenges that require someone with experience, courage, and demonstrated judgment to properly execute the role.

Much has been written about this "perilous" aspect of the General Counsel role,[1] and we think it is sufficiently important to merit some additional discussion here. More than fifteen years

1. See *Indispensable Counsel,* Introduction, *supra* note 2, at 10. See also, E. Norman Veasey & Christine Di Guglielmo, *General Counsel Buffeted by Compliance Demands and Client Pressures May Face Personal Peril,* 68 The Business Lawyer, 57 (2012); and Simmons & Dinnage, Introduction, *supra* note 3, at 81 ("Most of the debate surrounding in-house counsel clusters around issues of independence and ethics for the purpose of analyzing the willingness and capacity of in-house counsel to perform their multiple roles, particularly gatekeeping.")

ago, a noted legal ethics scholar commented that "the role of corporate counsel is among the most complex and difficult of those functions performed by lawyers."[2] This statement was made long before the era of Enron and WorldCom and other corporate scandals that led to heightened scrutiny of the General Counsel role as well as federal regulation of attorney professional conduct under the Sarbanes-Oxley Act.[3] More recently, the risks to General Counsel have been further increased as a result of additional regulation (e.g., the Dodd-Frank Act), increased investor activism, politics, influence of mainstream and social media and the impact of globalization. As a result, "the CLO is increasingly exposed to outside scrutiny and potential exposure to liability, prosecution, regulatory constraints, disbarment, and reputational harm."[4] And, of course, there is the ever-present risk that a General Counsel who clashes with other members of senior management—particularly the CEO—will lose her job.

Ignorance is No Excuse

In 2007, the Association of Corporate Counsel published a report (referred to here as the ACCA Report) concerning liability risks for in-house counsel, which includes many examples of General Counsel who have faced civil and criminal liability for

2. Geoffrey C. Hazard, Jr., *Ethical Dilemmas of Corporate Counsel,* 46 Emory L.J. 1011 (1997).

3. Part 205 of the SEC rules adopted pursuant to Section 307 of the Sarbanes-Oxley Act establish "minimum standards of professional conduct for attorneys appearing and practicing before the Commission in the representation of an issuer." 17 C.F.R. § 205.1. The rules define "appearing and practicing before the Commission" very broadly, encompassing any attorney providing advice to a client with respect to any matter described in an SEC filing. *Id.* § 205.2(a)(1).

4. Veasey & Di Guglielmo, *supra* note 1, at 60.

their actions.[5] Among the conclusions stated in that report were that "liability has increasingly been imposed or sought against in-house lawyers, particularly by the Securities and Exchange Commission (SEC) and federal prosecutors."[6] Though the report details some fairly egregious acts of in-house counsel misconduct, which evoke little sympathy for those who perpetrated them, it also includes examples of misdeeds more closely resembling negligence than intentional misconduct.

The ACCA Report includes several examples of in-house lawyers who were caught up in the option backdating scandal, which led to most of the enforcement activity against General Counsel and other in-house lawyers by the SEC in 2007. It is perhaps worth noting that backdating of stock options had been common practice for some time, especially among technology companies, before it became a favorite target of the SEC's Enforcement Division. In fact, according to the ACCA Report, many of ACCA's members reported that several top compensation consultants and outside auditors had blessed the practice of backdating. That, coupled with General Counsel's reliance on their CFOs to ensure appropriate accounting treatment, led to many General Counsel not questioning the practice of option backdating.[7] Lending additional credence to the view that the actions of many in-house counsel in these cases involved conduct that was negligent rather than intentional, the ACCA Report also notes:

> Right or wrong, many lawyers back off, or ignore the detailed analysis, when they are told that the CFO or auditors have blessed a deal. And this practice is one that can't be afforded

5. Association of Corporate Counsel, *In-House Counsel in the Liability Crosshairs* (Sept. 2007) [hereinafter *The ACCA Report*].

6. *Id.* at 5.

7. *Id.* at 31.

> any longer. Many in-house lawyers don't focus on examining or re-thinking what has been presented as an appropriate accounting treatment or acceptable accounting practice. *Indeed, many lack the compensation expertise and financial skills required to second-guess something that has been presented as acceptable in another suitably expert professional's judgment.*[8]

The SEC's pursuit of Google, Inc. and its former General Counsel, David Drummond, for Google's failure to register more than $80 million worth of stock options granted to Google employees and consultants in the two years prior to Google's IPO is arguably another instance of lack of knowledge leading to serious consequences for a prominent General Counsel. According to the facts set forth in the SEC's order, Drummond was aware that the registration and financial disclosure obligations to recipients of the stock options had been triggered but believed that Google could avoid providing the information to its employees by relying on an exemption from the registration requirements. He also failed to inform the Board of Directors that there were risks in relying on the exemption, which, in fact, was not available. To settle the charges, Google and Drummond agreed to a cease-and-desist order.[9]

The risk that ignorance of accounting or other rules or incorrect legal advice could become the basis for a securities law claim understandably became a significant cause for concern for General Counsel. To mitigate that risk, General Counsel are advised to learn the rules, make sure they have all relevant information necessary to give their advice, and seek expert guidance when appropriate. Good advice, but easier said than done

8. *Id.* (emphasis added)

9. *In the Matter of Google, Inc. and David C. Drummond*, Securities Act Release No. 8523 (Jan. 13, 2005), http://www.sec.gov/litigation/admin/33-8523.htm.

in fast-paced corporate environments where the expectation is for a rapid response from a General Counsel who knows all the answers. Nonetheless, General Counsel must be careful not to let those expectations result in taking shortcuts or engaging in "drive-by lawyering," particularly with respect to areas involving significant risks to the business.

Peril from the Server Room

Even for a General Counsel who is well versed in the rules, the demands of the role can lead to serious missteps. One of the more famous examples of this involved Ron Perelman's 2005 lawsuit against Morgan Stanley for allegedly misleading him about the financial stability of Sunbeam in order to seal a lucrative investment banking deal. The court awarded Perelman $1.45 billion in compensatory and punitive damages.[10] Donald Kempf, General Counsel of Morgan Stanley, resigned soon thereafter. A 2006 American Lawyer article, critical of the Morgan Stanley legal team's performance in the case, characterized Kempf as "distracted."[11]

One of the critical factors in this case, which has fueled the electronic discovery industry, was Morgan Stanley's inability to produce backup tapes containing thousands of emails that were potentially relevant to the case. The trial court judge referred to this a "willful and gross abuse of discovery obligations."[12] If not for this eDiscovery misstep, the outcome of the case likely would have been quite different. The case was, among other things, a serious wake-up call that something as mundane as a company's

10. The judgment was later reversed on appeal. *Morgan Stanley & Co. Incorporated v.Coleman (Parent) Holdings Inc.*, 955 So.2d 1124 (2007).

11. Susan Beck, *Recipe for Disaster,* The American Lawyer, at 88 (April 2006).

12. *Id.*

information technology disaster recovery strategy can impact the job stability of a General Counsel.

Close, but Not Too Close

The aspiration of every successful in-house lawyer is to be "close to the business," but is it possible to be too close? There is a wide array of choice between "go[ing] native as a yes-person for the business side and be[ing] legally or ethically compromised, or be[ing] an inveterate naysayer excluded from corporate activity."[13] But it can sometimes be challenging to strike the right balance, even in organizations with a strong emphasis on ethical behavior. Human nature and the desire to be part of the team can sometimes push the well-intended General Counsel over the line into the "yes-person" or enabler category.

Illustrating one extreme on this continuum, we find the story of Franklin Brown, the former General Counsel of Rite-Aid. Brown was convicted in 2003 of making false statements to the SEC, obstruction of justice, and tampering with a witness, all stemming from alleged misconduct in connection with an internal investigation and related investigations by the SEC and FBI that followed Rite Aid's $1.6 billion restatements of its earnings for 1997 to 1999.[14]

Though it is impossible to excuse the alleged conduct that led to Brown's convictions, which included bribing his secretary to backdate contracts, his motivations may make him a somewhat more sympathetic character. He had been General Counsel to Rite Aid for almost four decades and had provided legal advice not only to the company but also to the company's founder and

13. Heineman, Ch. 6, *supra* note 53, at 1.

14. Eriq Gardner, *The Ties that Bind,* Corp. Counsel (Oct. 2003), at 17–18.

the founder's son. He was described as deeply loyal to the company and these executives.[15] It was this excessive and misguided sense of loyalty, rather than personal gain, that apparently drove him to take the actions leading to his legal problems.

The Franklin Brown example, which involves a General Counsel actively participating in and concealing corporate misconduct to "protect" his client, is a difficult one to relate to. But every General Counsel faces situations involving disagreements with the CEO and/or peers about the advisability of a proposed course of action. Those situations can also create considerable pressure for a General Counsel to conform her advice to what the business wants to hear.

Residing in Two Worlds

How does a General Counsel navigate the boundaries of being a lawyer (which may require her to say "no") and still manage to stay a partner to the business? We asked this question of Knowledge Universe's Elizabeth Large, who has had considerable success in becoming a trusted advisor to the business. She told us that she has worked hard to be a partner to the business and earn the trust of other senior executives, but she also understands the importance of maintaining her objectivity and "pushing back" when appropriate. Indeed, her CEO and peers regularly seek her opinion on issues, but they also "expect the push back" on issues creating legal risk. She attributes achieving this balance in large part to her focus on "tone and culture" in the delivery of her advice to the business. She told us that "to be the best kind of lawyer you can be, you have to understand that the tone with which you deliver advice must be one that makes compliance with that advice more likely." Her comments reflect mastery of a

15. *Id.*

skill that is difficult for many people—knowing how to disagree without being disagreeable.

Large understands the challenges that exist for lawyers who may be too eager to please or too easily intimidated when their advice is challenged and says that she often sees this with more junior lawyers who are new to the organization. She coaches them to think independently, maintain their objectivity, and to understand that it is their obligation to raise concerns when they see them—if not directly to the client, to her as the General Counsel.

Know Which Hat You Are Wearing

As we discussed in Chapter Seven, today's General Counsel is expected to wear many hats, by which we mean the General Counsel must be knowledgeable on a wide range of subjects to properly execute the role. Here, we refer to "different hats" in another context, one that relates to the increased risk that a General Counsel may assume by explicitly taking on nonlegal roles. The ACCA Report highlights this issue, noting that:

> Regulators, prosecutors, and courts appear to be putting corporate counsel under the microscope for their conduct in connection with activities where corporate counsel have worn a nonlegal hat, sometimes heightening the ordinary expectations and duties of that nonlegal role to include the lawyer's legal training and knowledge. Obviously, this may increase the risks of such dual roles both for the lawyer and the client.[16]

On the other hand, the ACCA Report also notes that, regardless of whether they officially assume non-legal responsibilities,

16. *The ACCA Report, supra* note 5, at 7.

corporate counsel are increasingly expected to be knowledgeable about "their company's finances, lines of business, and operational strategies, and the business implications of questions and decisions that the lawyer may address only tangentially."[17]

Our observation is that these liability concerns do not appear to dissuade General Counsel from assuming non-legal roles. Most of the General Counsel we interviewed also have non-legal responsibilities and many hold or have held significant business roles while continuing to act as General Counsel. However, they are aware of the risks and take affirmative steps to manage them, the most important of which is to be clear about which hat they are wearing. This serves to protect them as well as their clients.

As a former litigator, Elizabeth Large understands the importance of being clear about whether she is giving legal or business advice. She recalls from her days as a litigator "grilling an in-house lawyer trying to get him to admit he was giving business advice" so she could destroy his claim of privilege. She commented that this is one of the reasons she always considers carefully which hat she is wearing and will often explicitly clarify for others when she is giving legal rather than business advice. She believes doing this "helps to increase her credibility" and finds that other members of the leadership team appreciate her efforts to be clear about her role.

Recent history indicates that these issues are challenging ones that should be on the minds of General Counsel as they execute their roles. The advice given by our interviewees about how to move from a General Counsel to a Generalist Counsel is equally relevant to navigating these challenges, particularly as it relates to building relationships and demonstrating leadership. But most important is having a strong ethical compass and the courage to do the right thing.

17. *Id.* at 8.

10

Implications of the Evolution

We believe the evolution of the General Counsel role has some important implications, not only for General Counsel but also for a variety of other stakeholders. We explore some of those implications in this final chapter.

For General Counsel (and Those Aspiring to the Role)

The story of the General Counsel role over the past fifty years has been one of increasing prominence, power, and prestige, perhaps surpassing the earlier heights it enjoyed during the golden age of General Counsel. At the same time, the role has grown increasingly more complex and demanding as General Counsel attempt to meet heightened expectations from both internal and external constituencies, which sometimes may be in conflict. Internally, CEOs have come to expect from General Counsel, among other things, a high degree of business acumen and strategic thinking. Meanwhile, globalization, increased regulation, and heightened scrutiny by regulators, investor activism, more litigation, media attacks, and other corporate reputational concerns are some of the external forces that may come into play, creating obstacles to the General Counsel's mission to help move the business forward. No one expects this landscape to become any less complex any time soon.

Need for Continuous Improvement

General Counsel will continue to be called upon to meet today's greater challenges and those that will arise in the future within the confines of the budget constraints that are an ever-present reality, requiring them to better manage legal costs. They will also increasingly internalize the continuous improvement mentality that the business now demands from all disciplines. We believe these factors will cause General Counsel to continue to look for ways to accomplish their work more efficiently, which will accelerate the trend toward disaggregation of legal services and the use of technology to more efficiently do work that is nonstrategic, can be routinized, and/or can be done more cost-effectively by more economically priced workers. The good news is that this evolution is something that Chief Information Officers, Chief Financial Officers, and other members of the executive team have previously faced. As such, the General Counsel will have many opportunities for "birds of a feather" discussions with their peers. These dynamics will continue to impact the relationships between in-house legal departments and their outside law firms, as well as many other facets of the legal services industry, as is discussed in more detail below.

Profile of Today's GC Candidate

The combination of increasing complexity and increased expectations also has implications for the profile of General Counsel candidates as well as competition for legal talent. Historically, the General Counsel position was relatively stable, and General Counsel tended to move relatively infrequently. However, in recent years, the turnover of General Counsel in large companies has significantly increased, and one of the principal factors has been the increased tendency of companies to recruit General

Counsel with prior experience in that role. Though leading executive search firms continue to suggest that law firm partners may be suitable candidates for these roles, the emphasis on breadth of experience, business acumen, and leadership and managerial skills make it more likely that someone with prior General Counsel experience—or at least in-house experience—will have the inside track. On a more positive note for outside counsel, we concur with the observations of at least one legal scholar that the increased mobility of General Counsel may create opportunity for outside counsel who have primary relationships to recapture their former role of providing institutional memory for their clients.[1]

A Note of Caution

Though we generally view as positive the General Counsel's increasing identification with the business, we think it is possible to carry that change in consciousness too far. We believe there is significant value and social utility in the General Counsel preserving a dual identity as a lawyer and a businessperson and maintaining the independence necessary to permit the General Counsel to effectively serve as a guardian of the corporation's integrity and reputation. Closer identification with the business does not obviate the need for the General Counsel to continue to be a lawyer.

For Outside Law Firms and Their Relationships with General Counsel

The evolution of the General Counsel role has both positive and negative implications for outside law firms, but we believe the

1. See Wilkins, Ch. 1, *supra* note 7, at 2095.

implications are largely positive if law firms are willing to seize some of the opportunities change creates.

More Sophisticated Clients; More Scrutiny

Clients of law firms today are much more sophisticated consumers of legal services and understand that a one-size-fits-all approach to problems that have a legal element does not make sense. They have become better educated about how to value different kinds of work as well as more efficient and cost-effective ways to get work done. This is unlikely to change. These clients will continue to press law firms to justify costs and delve into specifics of internal firm processes designed to ensure that law firms are delivering legal services as cost effectively as possible.[2] An example of this is the recent and well-publicized effort by Kia Motors to ensure technology proficiency by administering a technology test to prospective outside counsel.[3] This may be a somewhat extreme example, but it does illustrate that clients will not simply take for granted that law firms are taking appropriate steps to meet their needs as cost-efficiently as possible.

Law Firms Should Accept/Embrace Change

Some law firms—principally large firms with powerful clients who have demanded change—have responded to these demands by using methods similar to those employed by their corporate clients to reduce costs of legal service delivery (e.g., process

2. See *id.*, at 2110–11 (noting that corporate clients are increasingly looking at law firm internal structure and practices, citing as an example Wal-Mart, which in 2007 "began asking the firms on its preferred provider list whether the 'partners' working on the company's matters actually have an equity stake in the firm.")

3. See Monica Bay, *Tech Drive*, Law Technology News, at 19 (Dec. 2012).

improvement, outsourcing, downsourcing,[4] and technology innovations). However, although recent law firm survey data indicates that the vast majority of firms recognize that the game has changed, very few of them have actually taken affirmative steps to demonstrate this recognition to their clients. We think there is real opportunity here for law firms to gain a competitive advantage by engaging in open dialogue with their clients about these issues and partnering to find solutions that will be value added for both parties. Regardless of external pressure, we see no downside to law firms embracing project management and process improvement as disciplines to further their business goals.

There has been much discussion about the adversarial dynamics that exist between many companies and their outside counsel as General Counsel seek to use their purchasing power to pressure firms for discounts in fees, refuse to pay for associate training, and bring myriad other pressures to bear, while law firms largely fail to respond and seem paralyzed by fear of the future. However, it is abundantly clear from our conversations with General Counsel that there are models for positive relationships with outside counsel, which involve give-and-take and attempts to align incentives so that both sides can benefit.

Great(er) Expectations

As General Counsel have been required to step up their game as businesspeople, expectations of outside counsel have increased accordingly. Clients have greater expectations of outside counsel to help them provide business-oriented solutions and not just legal advice. This requires that outside counsel make an effort to

4. See Burk & McGowan, Ch. 3, *supra* note 31, at 5 (describing "downsourcing" as moving more routine work in litigation or transactions from full-cost associates to contract lawyers, legal specialists, or other lower-cost staff.)

learn the client's business so that legal advice can be given in a business context. Firms who are willing to invest their own time and resources in learning the client's business will have a competitive advantage.

In addition to learning the business, outside lawyers must learn to translate legal advice into corporate processes. General counsel and their legal departments are engaged in triage, meaning they don't have time to sort through mountains of difficult to decipher communications from outside counsel and spend even more time translating the recommended actions into something that is actionable by the business. If a law firm can help their in-house clients get closer to the business and remove process administrivia that prevents these clients from focusing on the substantive issues of law and the business, the law firm is much more likely to prevail in this increasingly competitive environment.

Other Players in the Legal Services Market

The trends toward applying business process discipline, disaggregation, and increasing use of technology to gain efficiency in corporate legal departments has spawned an industry of legal services providers other than law firms. These include legal process outsourcing vendors, both offshore and domestic; eDiscovery service providers; and software vendors selling e-billing products, and contract management, knowledge management, and compliance solutions, as well as consulting and professional services firms to help guide the General Counsel through the oftentimes complex maze of issues arising in connection with selection and implementation of these solutions.

Most importantly, lawyers, both in-house and in law firms will realize (or, in some cases, further embrace) that nonlawyers are and will continue to be critical elements of the legal services delivery system and designing business processes that include lawyers, paraprofessionals, technocrats, business analysts, domain expert consultants, and other "nontraditional" colleagues will help them succeed. Yes, law firms will have to share in the economics, but there will be better economics to share.

Legal Education

There has been a plethora of articles in recent years castigating law schools for their irresponsibility and greed for continuing to sell an overpriced legal education to record numbers of debt-ridden law students in the face of increasingly dismal employment prospects. Even before the forces of the most recent recession fueled the transformation of the job market, the supply of well-trained lawyers with specialized skills acquired from law firm training was at an all-time high, which has further diminished the willingness of clients to subsidize the training of new law firm lawyers.

The oversupply of firm lawyers relative to demand is not expected to change any time soon. Improvements in the economy may help to absorb the oversupply somewhat, but the economic forces that are eliminating or moving the work that lawyers used to do to lower cost service providers will continue to significantly impact the market.

These forces will undoubtedly impact the market for legal education. While law school admissions were at all-time highs just prior to and during the early part of the latest recession despite what now seems like the fairly obvious "handwriting on the wall," they have declined fairly significantly since then, and that trend is expected to continue. Competition among law schools for the reduced supply of applicants is expected to intensify, particularly among the vast majority of schools who do not enjoy "super elite" status.

Need and Opportunity for Change

Law schools have for some time faced considerable criticism for their failure to properly prepare their graduates to be legal practitioners. As clients became more vocal about their unwillingness to continue paying the freight for the apprenticeship model that allowed young lawyers to receive all their practical training in law firms, firms began to exert more pressure on law schools to bear some responsibility for this practical training. Although some law schools have responded by offering clinical programs and practical skills training, these programs remain marginalized by most law schools and are generally not considered an enhancement to an institution's academic reputation and ranking in the institutional hierarchy.

We think the current economic conditions, coupled with the increasing influence of the in-house bar, is also likely to be the catalyst for more rapid change in legal education. The failures of law schools to adequately prepare their graduates are even more pronounced when viewed through the lens of in-house practice. Courses such as accounting and finance rarely appear in law school curricula, and standard business courses such as contracts and corporations focus exclusively on "the law" without helping students understand how these disciplines affect business decisions. Courses in other areas critical to developing successful in-house lawyers (and, in our opinion, law firm lawyers), such as leadership, project management, and technology are virtually nonexistent. We see this as an opportunity for enterprising institutions to compete in the new world order of legal education.

Biographies

Peter Bragdon, Senior Vice President, Legal and Corporate Affairs, General Counsel, Secretary, Columbia Sportswear

Peter Bragdon received his B.A. in political science from Amherst College, a Masters of Studies in Law from Yale University, and his J.D. from Stanford Law School in 1993. He served as a political journalist for the *Congressional Quarterly* from 1984 to 1990 and also worked for the *St. Petersburg Times* before joining the Portland office of Stoel Rives LLP in 1993 as an associate in the corporate securities and finance group. While on a leave of absence from Stoel Rives, Mr. Bragdon served as Special Assistant Attorney General for the Oregon Department of Justice for seven months in 1996. He joined Columbia Sportswear in 1999 as Senior Counsel and Director of Intellectual Property. While on a leave of absence from Columbia, he served as Chief of Staff in the office of Oregon Governor Kulongoski from January 2003 through June 2004. He became Vice President, General Counsel, and Secretary of Columbia in July 2004 and was named Senior Vice President of Legal and Corporate Affairs, General Counsel, and Secretary in January 2010. He serves on the boards of the Outdoor Industry Association and the World Federation of Sporting Goods Industries. He also serves as a commissioner for the Port of Portland and is on the advisory council for All Hands Raised, a Portland, Oregon, based nonprofit organization with a mission of championing education, equity, and excellence for children from cradle to career.

James Dalton, former Senior Vice President, Corporate Development, General Counsel, and Secretary, Tektronix Inc.
James Dalton earned his B.A. in economics from the University of Massachusetts, Amherst, and received his J.D. from Boston College Law School in 1985. He worked as an associate for Black Helterline LLP, a Portland, Oregon, law firm, from 1985 until 1989, when he left to join the legal department at Tektronix, Inc. Dalton held a variety of positions at Tektronix and became its Vice President, General Counsel, and Secretary in 1997. He also served as Vice President of Corporate Development and was promoted to Senior Vice President in 2005. While at Tektronix, he chaired the Tektronix Foundation, as well as the boards of certain subsidiaries. He remained with Tektronix until the company was sold to Danaher Corporation in 2007. In 2003, he was appointed by Oregon's governor to the Board of the Oregon Public Employee Retirement System and served as Chair from 2009 until his resignation in 2012. He has also served on the boards of other for-profit and nonprofit organizations.

Henry Hewitt, Senior Counsel, Stoel Rives LLP
Henry Hewitt received his B.A. from Yale University and his J.D., *summa cum laude,* from Willamette University College of Law in 1969. Following his graduation from law school, he joined the predecessor firm to Stoel Rives LLP, where he became a partner in 1975. His practice emphasizes general business advice, acquisitions, financings, and corporate governance. He served as chair of Stoel Rives from 1989 to 1999 and again from 2002 to 2005. He led the firm's Business Services Practice Group from 2005 to 2009. During his career, he has been the principal legal advisor to the boards of directors of Tektronix, PacifiCorp, Fred Meyer, Electro Scientific Industries, Sequent Computer Systems, Medford Corporation, and other public and privately-owned companies. He has served on the boards of a number of for-profit and nonprofit entities and has received numerous honors and awards for his professional achievements as well as his civic and charitable contributions.

Richard Josephson, Senior Vice President, General Counsel, and Secretary, Schnitzer Steel Industries, Inc.
Rich Josephson received his B.A. in psychology from Case Western Reserve University and his J.D. from Marshall Wythe Law School at the College of William & Mary in 1972. Following graduation, he spent a year as a law clerk for the Honorable John D. Butzner of the U.S. Court

of Appeals for the Fourth District in Richmond, Virginia. In 1973, he joined the predecessor firm to Stoel Rives LLP in Portland, Oregon, as an associate. During his thirty-two years at Stoel Rives, he was named partner, established the firm's bankruptcy law practice, and represented clients in mergers and acquisitions and complex financial matters. Josephson represented bondholders of the Rose Garden sports arena in Portland in his final bankruptcy case for Stoel Rives, guiding the transfer of control of the Rose Garden from Portland Trailblazers basketball team owner Paul Allen to the investors. He served as a director of Portland Arena Management, the entity that manages the Rose Garden, from 2006 to 2008. He joined Schnitzer Steel in 2006 as Vice President, General Counsel, and Secretary.

Jeffrey B. Kindler, Former Chairman and Chief Executive Officer of Pfizer Inc.

Jeff Kindler received a B.A., *summa cum laude,* from Tufts University, followed by his J.D., *magna cum laude,* from Harvard Law School in 1980. After completing his degree, Kindler joined the Federal Communications Commission as an attorney. He served as a law clerk for Judge David L. Bazelon of the U.S. Court of Appeals of the D.C. Circuit and also for then U.S. Supreme Court Justice William J. Brennan, Jr. He practiced civil and criminal litigation at the Washington D.C. firm of Williams & Connolly, where he became a partner. In 1990, he joined the General Electric Company as Vice President of Litigation and Legal Policy. In 1996, he joined McDonald's Corporation as Executive Vice President and General Counsel, later becoming president of McDonald's Partner Brands. He joined Pfizer as Executive Vice President and General Counsel in 2002, and prior to his appointment as CEO in July 2006, he served as a Vice Chairman of the company. He retired from his position as Chairman and CEO of Pfizer in 2010. Currently, he is a senior advisor to Paragon Pharmaceuticals, a Venture Partner at Lux Capital, a leading venture capital firm, and a Director at Starboard Capital Partners, LLC. He serves as a trustee of Tufts University, the National Center on Addiction and Substance Abuse at Columbia University, the Manhattan Theatre Club, and President Obama's Management Advisory Board.

Margaret D. Kirkpatrick, Senior Vice President and General Counsel, Northwest Natural Gas Company

Margaret Kirkpatrick received her B.A. from The College of Wooster and received her J.D. from Northwestern School of Law of Lewis &

Clark College in 1982. Following graduation, she clerked for Judge W. Michael Gillette on the Oregon Court of Appeals. She joined the Portland, Oregon, office of Stoel Rives LLP in 1983 and was named a partner in 1991. She also received her LL.M. from the University of Edinburgh in 1987. At Stoel Rives, Ms. Kirkpatrick specialized in land use, natural resources, and environmental law. She represented Stoel Rives client NW Natural in a number of matters, including permitting of facilities and legislative changes and joined the company as Vice President and General Counsel in 2005. She has been a Director of Northwest Gas Association since November 16, 2010, and serves on the boards of a number of other organizations. She has also served as an adjunct professor at the Northwestern School of Law at Lewis & Clark College.

Hilary K. Krane, Vice President, General Counsel, and Corporate Affairs, NIKE, Inc.
Hilary Krane earned a B.A. from Stanford University and a J.D. from the University of Chicago in 1989. After graduating from law school, she clerked for Judge Milton Shadur, of the District Court for the Northern District of Illinois and then joined the Chicago office of Skadden, Arps, Slate, Meagher and Flom as a litigation associate where she focused on complex commercial litigation. She joined Price Waterhouse (now PwC) as a litigation attorney in 1994, served as an Assistant General Counsel there from 1996 to 2005, and became a partner in 2000. In 2006, she joined Levi Strauss & Co., where she served as served as General Counsel and Senior Vice President for Corporate Affairs. In 2010, she joined Nike Inc. as Vice President and General Counsel. In 2011, her responsibilities at Nike were expanded to include Corporate Affairs.

Eva Kripalani, Owner, Eva Kripalani Legal and Consulting Services
Eva Kripalani received her B.S., *magna cum laude,* from Portland State University and her J.D., *magna cum laude,* from Willamette University College of Law. Following graduation, she clerked for Judge Jonathan U. Newman on the Oregon Court of Appeals and then joined the Portland office of Stoel Rives LLP as an associate in 1987. She spent a decade at Stoel Rives, where her practice emphasized corporate law and mergers and acquisitions, and became a partner in 1994. In 1997, she joined KinderCare Learning Centers, Inc., as Vice President, General Counsel, and Corporate Secretary and was later promoted to Senior Vice President. Following the acquisition of KinderCare by Knowledge

Learning Corporation in 2005, she served as Senior Vice President and General Counsel of Knowledge Learning Corporation (now Knowledge Universe-US) and was promoted to Executive Vice President in 2006. After leaving Knowledge Learning Corporation, she founded a legal and business consulting firm. In collaboration with The Sumati Group, she provides guidance to corporations and law firms in areas such as law department management, corporate governance, ethics and compliance, and business process domains such as contract management. She serves on the boards of a number of nonprofit organizations and is a coauthor of this book.

Stephen K. Krull, Executive Vice President, General Counsel, and Corporate Secretary of Con-way Inc.

Steve Krull earned his B.S. in Business Administration from Eastern Illinois University and received his J.D. from Chicago-Kent College of Law, where he graduated with high honors and served as an editor of the *Kent Law Review*. Following law school, Mr. Krull joined Sidley Austin LLP in its Chicago office, where he specialized in commercial and banking transactions. He later became corporate counsel for A.B. Dick Company and joined Owens Corning in 1996. Over a fifteen-year career with Owens Corning, Mr. Krull held a variety of positions including Division Counsel, General Counsel, North American Building Materials; Vice President and General Counsel of Operations; and Vice President, Corporate Communications. He was named Senior Vice President, General Counsel, and Secretary of Owens Corning' in 2002, a position he held until he joined Con-way in April 2011. He has served on the boards of several nonprofit organizations and is currently Vice Chairman of the Board of St. Johns Jesuit Academy and High School in Toledo, Ohio. Most importantly, he was supported, encouraged, and tolerated from the first day of law school until today by his wife Beth.

Elizabeth Large, Executive Vice President and General Counsel, Knowledge Universe-US

Elizabeth Large received a bachelor's degree in economics and history from the University of Washington and a J.D. degree, *cum laude,* from Willamette University College of Law. After law school, she joined the Portland, Oregon, office of Stoel Rives, LLP as a member of the trial practice group. Elizabeth later joined the Special Litigation Unit at the Oregon Department of Justice, as an Assistant Attorney General, where she litigated constitutional challenges. Following that she established her own law practice, litigating complex civil cases in Oregon, Washington, and California for business, government, and individuals. She joined Knowledge Universe in 2005 as Assistant General Counsel and has served as General Counsel since 2009. She oversees the operations of the Legal Department, as well as Government Relations. She has a strong interest in serving our local community, with a special focus on literacy. She is currently a volunteer reader and board member for SMART (Start Making a Reader Today).

Nicholas Latrenta, former Executive Vice President and General Counsel, MetLife, Inc.

Nicholas Latrenta received a B.B.A. degree, *summa cum laude*, in Business Administration from the College of Insurance and a J.D. degree, *cum laude*, from Seton Hall Law School in 1979. He joined the company in 1969 as a trainee in the personal life insurance administration department and held several leadership positions over his career. In 1991, he was appointed Vice President and Secretary of the company after previously serving in key roles in MetLife's Strategic Research Group, which was responsible for researching and making recommendations on issues of strategic importance to the company and the company's international operations. He also served as a vice president in the actuarial department and held several positions in MetLife's law department. He oversaw a segment of MetLife's retirement and savings business from 1993 to 1996. In 1996, he was appointed Vice President in the Institutional Business Development and Compliance unit and was promoted to Senior Vice President in 1997. In 1999, he headed MetLife's International operations with responsibility for insurance operations in eleven countries outside the United States. From 2000 to 2004, he served as Senior Vice President, Institutional Business, where he was responsible for the management, product development and positioning of MetLife's group life, disability, dental, long-term care, and legal plans businesses and related marketing, planning, and business development activities. He then served as Chief Counsel for the company's Institutional Business, ERISA, and product tax legal group and Senior Chief Counsel for MetLife's insurance group, where he had oversight for legal matters related to U.S. and international business operations. He was appointed Executive Vice President and General Counsel of MetLife, Inc. in 2010, the position from which he retired in March 2013.

Bradley Lerman, Executive Vice President, General Counsel, and Corporate Secretary, Fannie Mae

Bradley Lerman received his B.A., *summa cum laude,* in economics from Yale University and his J.D., *cum laude,* from Harvard Law School in 1981. He served as an assistant U.S. attorney in the Northern District of Illinois from 1986 to 1994, holding various supervisory positions in the General Crimes, Major Crimes, and Special Prosecution divisions. In 1994, he joined the legal team headed by Independent Counsel Kenneth Starr in connection with the Whitewater investigation focusing on the real estate activities of President Bill Clinton and Hillary Clinton. Following that, he was a partner at two Chicago law firms: first at Kirkland & Ellis and later at Winston & Strawn. At Winston & Strawn he co-chaired the white-collar defense practice group. Prior to joining Fannie Mae in October 2012, Mr. Lerman was Senior Vice President, and Chief Litigation Counsel at Pfizer, Inc., where he was responsible for leading the company's product and commercial litigation, government investigations, and patent litigation teams. (He was at Pfizer when interviewed for this book.) He also had responsibility for Pfizer's Discovery Response Team, civil and criminal justice reform program, and the Pfizer Legal Alliance program. As Fannie Mae's Executive Vice President, General Counsel, and Corporate Secretary, Mr. Lerman oversees the Legal Department and Government and Industry Relations.

James L. Lipscomb, former Executive Vice President and General Counsel, MetLife, Inc.

James Lipscomb is a graduate of Howard University and Columbia University School of Law, where he received his J.D. in 1972. He later received his LL.M. from NYU Law School in 1977. He joined MetLife in 1972 as a real estate lawyer and practiced real estate law for nearly two decades. In 1989, he was chosen to join MetLife's in-house think tank created by the company's CEO to identify future business opportunities for MetLife. He served as part of this elite group for a year and a half before being asked to join the real estate investments department at MetLife. In 1997, Lipscomb was appointed head of the Corporate Planning and Strategy Department at MetLife where he served until 2000. From 2000 to 2001, Lipscomb served as President and CEO of Conning Corporation, then a MetLife subsidiary, where he was responsible for highly regulated investment activities. He returned to the law department as Deputy General Counsel in 2001 and became Executive

Vice President and General Counsel in 2003. He retired from MetLife in 2010, after thirty-eight years of service. During his career, Lipscomb wrote and lectured extensively on real estate and corporate mattes. Lipscomb is involved in a variety of charitable and civic activities, including Center of Hope (Haiti), Inc.

Marla S. Persky, Senior Vice President, General Counsel, and Corporate Secretary of Boehringer Ingelheim Corporation

Marla Persky received a B.S. from Northwestern University and her J.D. from Washington University School of Law in 1982. She joined the Chicago law firm Lurie, Sklar & Simon as a litigation associate following graduation. In 1986, she joined Baxter Healthcare Corporation, where she spent almost twenty years in various legal and business roles, including Corporate Counsel, Associate General Counsel and Chief Litigation Counsel, and General Manager of Althin Medical Inc. In 1994, she became General Counsel to Baxter's global business groups and then served as Acting General Counsel and Corporate Secretary for Baxter International Inc. from 2004 to 2005. She joined Boehringer Ingelheim Corporation in 2005 as Senior Vice President, General Counsel, and Corporate Secretary, where her responsibilities include providing strategic and business planning and development advice and advising the senior management in the U.S. and the German parent company on all U.S. legal issues facing the global company. She has served on the boards of for-profit and nonprofit organizations and has received numerous awards for her contributions in the field of diversity.

Mardilyn Saathoff, Vice President, Legal, Risk, and Compliance, NW Natural Gas Company

Mardilyn Saathoff, received her B.A., *magna cum laude,* and her Master of Arts in Teaching, *summa cum laude,* from Lewis & Clark College and her J.D., *cum laude,* from Lewis & Clark Law School in 1990. Following graduation from law school, she joined the Portland, Oregon, office of Stoel Rives LLP. At Stoel Rives, she focused her practice in corporate, securities, and finance. In 1996, she left Stoel Rives to work for Oregon's Department of Justice, where she supervised the business transactions section. In 2000, she joined Tektronix, Inc. as Senior Legal Counsel. In 2003, she was asked to join Oregon's Governor Kulongoski as his General Counsel and took a leave of absence from Tektronix. She remained on the governor's staff until 2005, also serving as his

Business and Economic Development Advisor. She returned to Tektronix in 2005 as Chief Compliance Officer and Assistant General Counsel. Following the acquisition of Tektronix by Danaher Corporation in 2007, she became Chief Compliance Officer for Danaher. In 2008, she joined NW Natural Gas Company as Chief Compliance Officer, Deputy General Counsel, and Corporate Secretary and was promoted to Vice President, Legal, Risk, and Compliance in 2013. Saathoff has also served on the boards of a number of nonprofit organizations.

Thomas Sabatino, Jr., Executive Vice President, General Counsel, and Corporate Secretary, Walgreen Co.
Thomas Sabatino, Jr. earned his B.A. from Wesleyan University and received his J.D. from the University of Pennsylvania in 1983. Following graduation, he worked for law firms for several years until he was recruited to the legal department of Baxter International in 1986. Sabatino served as Corporate Counsel for Baxter Healthcare Corporation from August 1986 to December 1990. He left Baxter to become President and Chief Executive Officer of Secure Medical, Inc., a small medical device company. In 1992, he joined American Medical International, Inc., and became Vice President and General Counsel in 1993. He returned to Baxter in 1995 and was promoted General Counsel of Baxter International in 1997. He remained at Baxter until 2004, when Schering-Plough Corporation hired him as Executive Vice President and General Counsel. In 2010, he joined United Airlines Inc. as General Counsel. Following the merger of United Airlines with Continental Airlines and the subsequent acquisition of U.S. Air, he served as Senior Vice President, General Counsel, and Corporate Secretary of UAL Corporation and United Continental Holdings Inc. He joined Walgreen Co. in September 2011 as Executive Vice President, General Counsel, and Corporate Secretary. Sabatino has also served on the boards of a number of nonprofit organizations.

Amy Schulman, Executive Vice President and General Counsel, Pfizer Inc., and Business Unit Lead, Pfizer Consumer Healthcare
Amy Schulman, a Phi Beta Kappa graduate of Wesleyan University, earned her J.D. from Yale Law School in 1989. Prior to joining Pfizer, Schulman was a partner at the law firm DLA Piper, where she served as a member of the Board and Executive Policy Committees and built and led the firm's mass tort and class action practice. Schulman joined Pfizer as General Counsel in June 2008 and was named head of Pfizer

Nutrition in 2010. She ran the nearly $2 billion global business from January 2011 until November 2012 when Pfizer completed its sale to Nestlé. In addition to serving as Executive Vice President and General Counsel, she also is the company's Business Unit Lead for Consumer Healthcare (a $4 billion global business) and is the executive sponsor of the company's Global Women's Council. She serves on the Board of Directors for both Wesleyan University and the Brooklyn Academy of Music.

Bradley J. Thies, Senior Vice President, General Counsel, and Secretary, FEI Company

Brad Thies received a B.A. in political science and history from Willamette University and a J.D. from Columbia Law School in 1986. After law school, he joined the Seattle office of Davis Wright Tremaine as an associate. In 1988, he joined the Portland, Oregon, office of Stoel Rives LLP. He left Stoel Rives to become General Counsel for one of his clients, Hometown Buffet, a restaurant company based in San Diego, California. Following the sale of HomeTown Buffet in 1998, Mr. Thies joined DataWorks Corporation, an enterprise website monitoring and analytics software company. In 1999, he returned to Oregon as General Counsel and Secretary of FEI Company, a diversified scientific instruments company based in Hillsboro, Oregon. He left FEI in 2000 to become General Counsel of WebTrends Corporation, an enterprise software company that developed, marketed, and sold website monitoring and analytics software. In 2001, he returned to FEI as Vice President, General Counsel, and Secretary and was promoted to Senior Vice President in 2011.

Elpidio "P.D." Villarreal, Senior Vice President—Global Litigation, GlaxoSmithKline

Elpidio ("P.D.") Villarreal is a Phi Beta Kappa graduate of Columbia University and received his J.D. from Yale Law School in 1985. He clerked on the United States Court of Appeals for the Seventh Circuit in Chicago for the late Honorable Luther M. Swygert, after which he joined the Chicago office of Latham and Watkins. He left there after a year to join the Chicago firm Sonnenschein, Nath & Rosenthal, where he became a partner and practiced until he was recruited by General Electric Company's legal department in 1995. There, he was instrumental in developing GE's Early Dispute Resolution Program, chaired GE's

Litigation Council, and led GE's Legal Department Diversity Initiative. He served as Senior Litigation Counsel when he left in 2005 to join Schering Plough as Vice President and Associate General Counsel, Litigation & Conflict Management. In 2009, he joined GlaxoSmithKline Senior Vice President-Global Litigation. He has received numerous awards for his contributions in the fields of civil rights and diversity.

Allen Waxman, Senior Vice President and General Counsel
Eisai, Inc.
Allen Waxman holds a B.A., *magna cum laude*, from Dartmouth College and a J.D., *magna cum laude*, from Harvard Law School in 1987. Upon graduating from law school, he clerked for the Honorable Thomas Penfield Jackson of the United States District Court for the District of Columbia. He joined Williams & Connolly, LLP, in 1989, where he became a partner and served as national counsel in pharmaceutical litigation. He left Williams & Connolly in 2002 and joined Pfizer as Senior Assistant General Counsel in 2003, where he was later promoted to General Counsel. He left Pfizer to join Kaye Scholer LLP in 2008, where he was a partner and chair of the firm's Life Sciences Group. In 2012, he joined Eisai Inc. as Senior Vice President and General Counsel. Waxman chairs the Board of Equal Justice Works, a national not-for-profit dedicated to mobilizing the next generation of lawyers into the public interest and also serves on the boards of a number of other nonprofit organizations. He previously served as Chair of the Board of Trustees for Thurgood Marshall Academy, a public charter high school in Washington, D.C.

Index